MW00810996

THAT YOU
MIGHT BELIEVE

THAT YOU MIGHT BELIEVE

Henry M. Morris

GOOD NEWS PUBLISHERS
Westchester, Illinois 60153

THAT YOU MIGHT BELIEVE
Copyright © 1978 by Henry M. Morris
All rights reserved.
Printed in the United States of America.
Library of Congress Catalog Card Number 78-68398
ISBN 0-89107-157-1

CONTENTS

FOREWORD

During my first pastorate in Houston, Texas, it was my privilege to meet and later welcome into the fellowship of the church a young instructor of civil engineering at Rice Institute named Henry M. Morris. Little did I realize then how that association would develop into a lasting mutual friendship embracing more than 30 years!

When Dr. Morris prepared his first draft of *That You Might Believe,* he invited me to read the manuscript, and make suggestions in the text. Later, the book was published, with gratifying results. Many believed as a result of that initial edition.

I am delighted now that our times demand a new enlarged edition. Once again, Dr. Morris has invited me to read the text, which I have done page by page. Admittedly, there are some things that are hard to understand because of my limited knowledge in the fields of science and archaeology. But I found adequate confirmation of many things which I have long known and believed as truth.

Dr. Morris is an honored and respected Bible scholar as well as a scientist whose handling of the great themes of Scripture and science is to be trusted. But above these, he is a man of God with one passion in his life and all his writings—that *you* might believe!

That is his prayer for this volume—and mine.

Richard H. Seume, D.D.,
Chaplain to the Seminary,
Dallas, Texas.

INTRODUCTION TO
THE REVISED EDITION

It is not often that the revised edition of a book is brought out a quarter of a century after the first edition has gone out of print, and it may seem presumptuous even to attempt such a thing. There have been so many requests for this, however, and I have heard from so many people over the years who were won to Christ through the first edition of *That You Might Believe*, that it finally seemed like the right thing to do. I can only hope and pray that the Lord will use this new edition as He used the first. In spite of its many deficiencies, that first book apparently spoke to both the minds and hearts of many people of the post-war era. There is a new generation now, but the same old needs still exist and the same age-old truths are still able to meet those needs.

Actually, the case for the truth of the Bible and Christianity is even stronger today than it was then. The Gospel of Christ has made a tremendous impact on the nation's campuses in the last 30 years, as well as on people in general. When I was writing the first edition back in 1944 and 1945, it was almost impossible to find a Bible-believing faculty member in any of the nation's secular universities. As a young instructor at Rice trying to establish an effective Christian witness for Christ on the campus, I found no colleagues of like mind on the faculty at all. The dearth of evangelicals on college faculties was almost universal at that time.

Now, however, one can find evangelicals on practically every university or college faculty, as well as from one to several strong Christian student groups. There will even be a few unashamed creationists on nearly every faculty today! It is wonderful to see what God has accomplished in these past three decades.

But, of course, real Christians are still a small minority, and there is still great need everywhere. Unbelief and immorality have become more open and extreme at the same time that the Christian faith has become more visible and effective. There is as great a need as ever for books which aggressively present the Gospel of Christ in clear and logical terms.

Another development has been the modern creationist movement. *That You Might Believe* was, so far as I know, the first book published since the Scopes trial in which a scientist from a secular university advocated recent special creation and a worldwide flood. Now, however, there are thousands of creationist scientists and the creationist revival has reached international proportions.

Consequently, this new edition of the book will be facing an environment significantly different from that of 30 years ago. However, the needs of people are still the same and the truth is still the same so the message of the book, though somewhat updated, is still the same message.

As a matter of fact, the book in one sense has never actually been out of print. *That You Might Believe* was first published in 1946 by Good News Publishers. It was then considerably enlarged and published in a different format by Moody Press in 1951 under the title *The Bible and Modern Science*. Soon after, it was drastically condensed and published as a paperback in the Moody Colportage Library in 1956. Despite further revisions, it has continued in this format ever since. This new edition is based mainly on the enlarged 1951 volume.

I am honored and happy that Good News Publishers will now be co-publishing this long-delayed second edition of the original title, *That You Might Believe*. Clyde Dennis, the founder of Good News, took a chance on an unknown author and an unusual book in 1946. I have written more than 25 books since that first one—sort of an occupational disease, I guess—but none has been more fruitful in terms of people won for the Lord. Mrs. Dennis and her sons have carried on the work of Good News Publishers since the death of Clyde Dennis, and I am very grateful for their desire to bring out a new edition, in cooperation with the Creation-Life Publishers.

I wish also to thank Dr. Richard Seume, Chaplain at Dallas Theological Seminary, for his gracious Foreword to this new edition. Dr. Seume was my pastor when the first edition was written and he reviewed the original manuscript. His fellowship and counsel through the years have been greatly appreciated. Special thanks also go to my mother, Mrs. I. H. Morris, for typing the manuscript, as she has done for so many of my other books. This has been a real labor of love at her age (78), especially with arthritis in her fingers, and she will certainly share in any ministry the book may have.

The changes in the new edition have been kept to a minimum consistent with the necessary updating. Since I am now over 30 years older than when the first book was written, I tend to express things somewhat differently today, but the thoughts themselves haven't changed too much. For the most part the book is essentially still the same.

That You Might Believe is not written as a technical treatise for scholars, but rather as a straightforward witness to ordinary people who need the Lord and who need evidence and assurance that his Word is true and his salvation is real. It is our prayer, as it was with the first edition 32 years ago, that the Lord will use it to bring many people to himself, through faith in the Lord Jesus Christ.

> Henry M. Morris
> San Diego, California
> January, 1978

THAT YOU
MIGHT BELIEVE

1

The day in which we are living might well be called
the Age of Confusion. Seemingly no realm of life has
escaped the turmoil and perplexity so characteristic of
these times. The almost hopelessly complex political
and international picture has its social and economic
counterpart in the apparently irreconcilable conflict
between capital and labor, in the fields of world trade
and finance, in racial conflicts, in seemingly every
phase of man's activity.

Crime and mental disturbances are increasing at
staggering rates—nowhere more than here in
America. Drunkenness, drug addiction and vice are
becoming epidemic as moral barriers fall on every
hand. Few people in the world seem to know or care
any more about the difference between wrong and
right. In fact, atheistic Communism has taken over
half the world, and there is an imminent danger that it
may soon conquer the rest of it.

Even in the revered domain of science, increased

knowledge seems to have brought increased confusion. The concepts of relativity, indeterminism, chance and uncertainty that now permeate scientific thinking have upset faith in the time-honored laws of physics, chemistry, and the other basic sciences. The Copernican system of astronomy and Newtonian mechanics and gravitation, which were long accepted as incontrovertibly proved and universally applicable, have been modified by Einstein's theories of relativity. The old ideas of matter and energy have undergone radical revision as a result of Einstein's theories and Planck's Quantum Theory.

There is a tendency now to interpret all scientific laws and facts in terms of probability and relativity. It is said that nothing can be completely understood or evaluated because of the impossibility of obtaining a point of reference whose position in both space and time is absolutely fixed and known. Consequently, all things must be viewed in relation to other things, which are themselves not completely understood, and it is impossible to realize the whole truth about anything.

The need for finding something "absolute" is not limited to the fields of physics and astronomy. If ever we needed something stable to which we could hold and some vantage point from which we could understand the real meaning behind all the confusion of life that time is today. It is unthinkable that our Creator God, if he exists, would have left us in this condition without providing something from which we could obtain understanding and certainty. That he did provide just such a Rock is the confident testimony of millions of men and women, not only in this age but in ages past.

This Rock is not only a creed or a philosophy; it is not merely a set of standards by which to live, or a scientific formula that reveals the workings of the universe. It is the Rock of Ages, the Lord Jesus Christ. He is "the way, the truth, and the life" (John 14:6). He is the only

Way that God has provided. He alone is complete and incarnate Truth. He is the only one who provides sure understanding of life and gives the only Life that is complete and satisfying and everlasting.

These things can be said only on the basis of faith. Faith in Christ and his Word permits me to say these things with complete assurance and conviction. I believe in the deity of the Lord Jesus Christ, his virgin birth, his substitutionary death on the cross of Calvary, his literal resurrection and ascension, and his promise that I have everlasting life through faith in him as my Savior and Lord. I believe that the Bible is the Word of God, literally inspired by the Holy Spirit, free from error of any sort, whether scientific, historical, or internal contradiction.

It is granted that those who believe these truths must grasp them by faith. They cannot be attained by reason alone. Because of this, it has become the custom in intellectual circles to dismiss them as outmoded beliefs, conceived in superstition and nurtured by scientific and philosophical illiteracy.

This charge, however, is very unreasonable. Many of the outstanding philosophers and scientists of the past and present have been and are Bible-believing Christians. There is a tremendous amount of objective evidence to support the belief that the Bible is the inspired Word of God, and that Jesus Christ is the Son of God and the eternal Savior of all who receive him into their lives by faith. The doctrine of the inspiration of the Scriptures is thoroughly compatible with all true science and reason and in no way does violence to common sense and intelligence. Some of the evidence for these great truths is set forth in the pages that follow.

Young people, for whom this book is primarily intended, are normally developing a critical and inquisitive mind regarding many things, not the least of which is the real meaning behind their own existence.

This book is written with the hope of strengthening the faith of young Christians and convincing others that the traditional Christian beliefs are founded on objective facts, not on superstition and ignorance. I have attempted to follow a reasonable and scientific approach, realizing, nevertheless, that the last and greatest step must be taken by faith.

The wide range in subject matter makes it impossible, in a book of this size, to include all the information pertinent to this subject. The bibliography at the end of the book includes the material used in preparing this book and is for those sufficiently interested in carrying the study further. Since books that oppose the Christian viewpoint can be found in large numbers in most university libraries, while those that support Christianity are scarce, it seemed unnecessary to include the former in these bibliographies.

Let us proceed, then, with a critical examination of the Bible and its claims.

MODERN SCIENCE
IN THE BIBLE

2

It is commonly supposed, even by most professing Christians, that the Bible contains much scientific error. Modern science and scholarship, particularly as represented by the concepts of evolution and biblical criticism, are the basis of liberalism in religion, humanism in education, and practical unbelief.

The Bible was obviously not intended primarily as a scientific textbook, but this does not justify the inference of possible scientific inaccuracy. If the book is really God-given, as it claims to be, it is unthinkable that it should contain scientific mistakes. Either it is scientifically accurate whenever it happens to touch on some phase of science or it is purely the product of human beings, and no better than any other book of ethics. I firmly believe the former to be the correct view.

One of the most arresting evidences of the inspiration of the Bible is the great number of scientific truths that were hidden within its pages for 30 centuries or more before scientists—working on their own in the last few centuries—discovered them. Let us look at a few of these.

Consider the field of astronomy. For thousands of years, many wise men occupied themselves with counting and identifying the stars and constellations. Before the invention of the telescope in the 17th century, the number of the stars was regarded as rather well determined. The great Ptolemy had given the number as 1056. Tycho Brahe catalogued 777 and Kepler counted 1005. This number has since been tremendously increased, of course, and the end is not yet even remotely in view. It is now known that there are well over 100 billions of stars in our own galaxy, with billions of other galaxies like our own. Verily, as all astronomers now agree, it is not humanly possible to count all the stars. This would not have been admitted by scientists a few centuries ago. But the Bible makes the assertion over and over again, as in Jeremiah 33:22, ". . .the host of heaven *cannot* be numbered."

It has long been contended by critics of the Scriptures that the Bible portrays the earth as the fixed center of the universe, around which the sun, planets, and stars revolve. Also, it is claimed that the earth is viewed as flat, supported in some mysterious way by foundations or pillars. References to "the ends of the earth" and "the foundations of the earth" are cited. An honest reading of such expressions, however, indicates the meaning is simply "the uttermost parts of the earth" in the one case and "the sub-crustal rocks of the earth" in the other. Furthermore, modern scientists and engineers today measure the motions of the sun and stars relative to the earth just as people did in Bible days.

The Bible often uses figures of speech, just as modern writers do, and this is always evident in the context when they do. There are no scientific mistakes in the Bible. On the contrary, there are many passages which indicate very modern concepts of astronomy.

For example, look at Job 26:7, "He hangeth the earth upon nothing." That sounds amazingly like 20th-century science! The force of gravity is said to account for the earth's affinity to the sun, but that explains nothing. No one knows what gravity is or why it is. It is merely a term invented to describe certain observed phenomena. Truly, there is nothing that modern science can add to or take away from the age-old statement that God has hung the earth upon nothing.

Or consider Isaiah 40:22, where, speaking of God, the prophet says: "It is he who sitteth upon the circle of the earth." The word translated "circle" is the Hebrew *khug,* a more exact connotation of which is "sphericity" or "roundness." Does that sound like a flat earth with four corners?

That Jesus knew the true shape of the earth and also the fact of its rotation upon its axis is inferentially evident from an examination of his words in Luke 17:34-36. He was speaking to his disciples about his second coming, which was to be instantaneous and would be seen by all at one and the same moment.

"I tell you in that night there shall be two in one bed; the one shall be taken and the other shall be left. Two women shall be grinding together; the one shall be taken and the other left. Two men shall be in the field; the one shall be taken and the other left."

He said that the great moment would come at night, while men sleep, but also in the early morning when women are grinding meal, and yet in midday, because that is when men are in the field. This is all quite reasonable to us because we know that the earth rotates on its axis and presents different areas to the light of the sun at different times. Obviously, it is quite possible for it to be night at one point on the earth, early morning at another point, and midday somewhere else—all at one and the same moment. But

Jesus was speaking scientific truth centuries before men discovered it.

The 19th Psalm is still a source of amusement to the critics. In speaking of the sun, the psalmist says: "His going forth is from the end of the heaven, and his circuit unto the ends of it: and there is nothing hid from the heat thereof." It was claimed that the writer of this verse obviously believed in the unscientific notion of the sun's revolving about the earth.

This charge is specious, however, since even scientists still use words and phrases of the same sort. From our natural viewpoint the sun does rise in the morning, move across the sky, and set in the evening. The whole science of nautical and engineering astronomy is based on the assumption, made purely for convenience, that the earth is the center of a great celestial sphere, moving along the surface of which in ordered paths are the sun, moon, planets, and stars. And as far as practical usage is concerned, this is so. On this assumption, courses can be plotted, positions determined, and scores of other applications made. As a matter of fact, since all motions must be measured relative to other points which are themselves in motion (neither the sun nor any other point in the universe is motionless, so far as we know), it is really more scientific (and more simple) to measure the movements of heavenly bodies relative to the earth in exactly this way.

It is now believed by leading astronomers that the sun, with the entire solar system in tow, actually does move through space at the tremendous speed of 720,000 miles per hour in such a gigantic orbit that it would require over two million centuries to complete it. Furthermore, our galaxy is undoubtedly moving with respect to other galaxies. Thus, as a matter of fact, the sun's circuit is from one end of the heavens to the other! Who can accuse the Holy Spirit of ignorance of astronomy?

It is glorious to realize that the Great Astronomer and Mathematician who created the heavens, setting all the stars and galaxies of stars in their appointed courses, and who, according to the 147th Psalm, "calls them all by their names," is the same one who calls you and me to eternal life in Jesus Christ!

But let us look into the science of meteorology for a moment. Water is precipitated as rain or snow and drained off by the river system into the ocean, where it is raised by evaporation back into the skies and carried by the wind back to the land again. The "water cycle" is a fundamental fact of this comparatively new field of science. Yet this fact was strikingly set forth in the Bible long before men discovered it. It is well known that the major wind currents of the world follow well-defined circuits. But this great truth is a matter of comparatively recent discovery. Now read what King Solomon wrote 3,000 years ago: "The wind goeth toward the south, and turneth about unto the north; it whirleth about continually, and the wind returneth again according to his circuits. All the rivers run into the sea, yet the sea is not full; unto the place from whence the rivers come, thither they return again" (Ecclesiastes 1:6, 7). No wonder men speak of the wisdom of Solomon! But isn't it pertinent to ask how he happened to know these things when no one else knew them until thousands of years later?

Also consider the words of Elihu in Job 36:27-29 (American Standard Version): "For he draweth up the drops of water, which distil in rain from the vapor thereof, which the skies pour down and drop upon man abundantly. Yea, can any understand the spreadings of the clouds, the thunderings of his pavilion?" This passage is a concise summary of those phases of the hydrologic cycle involving the marvelous physical processes of evaporation, condensation, and precipitation.

There is very much for science yet to learn concerning the details of the processes of the water cycle. Each phase of the cycle is quite necessary for life to exist on the earth, and offers abundant testimony to its origin at the hands of an infinitely wise and beneficent Creator.

There are many more references in Scripture to various phases of the sciences of hydrology and meteorology, all remarkably in accord with the most up-to-date studies in these fields.

Speaking of oceans, those who criticize the first chapter of Genesis should take note of the marvelous statement that "God said, Let the waters under the heaven be gathered together unto one place." We know, of course, that all the oceans and the great gulfs and seas of the world are joined together in one common bed, but how did Moses know it? He was acquainted with the waters of the Mediterranean Sea and the Red Sea, at least, which certainly had no immediate connection. He recognized this fact, too, mentioning that God called the gathering-together of the waters "seas" (more than one).

It is significant also that the medical and sanitary laws of Moses were very far in advance of their times. To see this, one need only compare the customs and beliefs of the ancient Egyptians and Babylonians with those of the Hebrews as given to them in the books of Moses. In the 11th chapter of Leviticus there is a list of animals, fishes, birds, and insects that the Israelites could regard as clean and fit to eat. The criterion of both chewing the cud and parting the hoof was set as a guide to the clean animals. The pig, the rabbit, and the hare were prohibited by this rule. It is known now that these latter animals are easily subject to parasitic infection and are safe only if they have been cleanly fed and well cooked before eating.

The birds and fish the Israelites were permitted to eat are now known to modern medical science as the safest and best. The only insects allowed for food were certain locusts, beetles, and grasshoppers, which are now known to be clean feeders and safe for human consumption. They are still eaten in large quantities in some parts of the world.

In Deuteronomy 14:21, Moses forbade the Jews to eat the flesh of any animal that had died a natural death. This is still regarded as such good advice that similar laws are in force in most civilized countries today.

Water supply and sewage disposal are subjects of great interest and import to both bacteriologists and engineers, as well as to the general public. It was not until a few years ago that the significance of a clean and sanitary water supply in the prevention of disease was recognized. But Moses seemed to understand something of modern bacteriology, because he forbade the drinking of water from small or stagnant pools, or from water that had been contaminated by animals or meat. (See Leviticus 11:29-36).

In Deuteronomy 23:12-14, directions were given for the disposal of human excreta by burial. All of these sanitary regulations, as well as those concerning the personal cleanliness of the body, were far ahead of the practices in even the advanced countries of the world until the past hundred years. This is true also of the prescribed segregation and treatment of such diseases as leprosy.

In the 25th chapter of Leviticus, it was decreed that all of the cultivated lands of the Israelites were to lie idle every seventh year. At first, this might have appeared unreasonable, in view of the great need for food, and yet modern agricultural science knows that it was a very wise provision. Even though crops are rotated from year to year, the land needs a rest every seven years. When this need is disregarded the land will eventually cease producing altogether. This is especially true of large areas that have been cleared of trees and other vegetation in order to plant more crops.

Not only were the scientific and medical laws of

Moses far ahead of their times, but so were the civil laws. The laws of Moses form the basis of the legal codes of all the great free nations of the world today. Although it is true that the early Babylonians and Hittites had codes of law similar in some respects to those of Moses, they were not nearly as reasonable, as just, or as complete, as those in the Pentateuch. The Hebrew law was unique in that it centered everything else in the worship and service of one God, Jehovah.

The great truth revealed in Leviticus 17:11 and a number of other Scriptures concerning the importance of blood in the biological mechanism, has only been adequately comprehended in recent years: "For the life of the flesh is in the blood, . . ."

Continuance of life depends upon the continued supply of oxygen, water, and food to the cells of all parts of the body. This absolutely necessary function is accomplished in a very marvelous manner by the blood which circulates constantly throughout the body. The function of blood in combating disease-producing organisms and in repairing injured tissues is one of the most significant discoveries of modern medical science. The use of blood transfusions as a treatment of disease further testifies to the supremacy of the blood in the life of the flesh.

The Word of God was scientifically accurate in this great biological truth thousands of years before men elaborated upon it. Yet it was given primarily to teach an even greater spiritual truth—the necessity for the shedding of blood in sacrifice for the remission of sins. The blood, which is the channel of life, becomes also the carrier of disease and infection through the body. Physical life symbolizes spiritual life, and physical death symbolizes spiritual death. Physical disease and injury symbolize the spiritual disease of sin.

As the infection of sin spreads throughout the soul, it will ultimately produce eternal spiritual death. If spiritual life is to be produced and maintained, new life

must be introduced from without to combat the rav-
ages of sin in the life. Figuratively speaking, a trans-
fusion of blood is essential, and it must be from a donor
whose blood possesses the purity and efficacy required
for the salvation of the spiritually dying soul.

This is the merest glimpse of the depths of spiritual
(and even biological) meaning in the biblical doctrine
of substitutionary sacrifice. "Without the shedding of
blood, there is no remission of sins" (Hebrews 9:22).
This was the symbolic meaning of the animal sacrifices
in Mosaic law. It finds its ultimate and universal cul-
mination in the sacrificial death of the Son of God for
the sins of the world. Jesus said: "This is my blood of
the new testament, which is shed for many for the
remission of sins" (Matthew 26:28).

By virtue of Jesus' atoning death, each one who receives by faith his life—poured out unto death, but
raised up again by the power of God—receives forgiveness and cleansing of all sin, and in fact receives Christ
himself. All this is symbolized by the shed blood. Jesus
said: "Whoso eateth my flesh, and drinketh my blood,
hath eternal life; and I will raise him up at the last
day. . . . He that eateth my flesh, and drinketh my
blood, dwelleth in me, and I in him" (John 6:54, 56).

Many other examples of scientific truth in Scripture
could be cited from practically every field of physical,
biological, or social science. But we will look at only
one more at this point.

The most basic principles of all science are those of
the conservation and deterioration of energy. The law
of energy conservation states that, in any transformation of energy in a closed system from one sort into
another, the total amount of energy remains unchanged. The law of mass conservation states that although matter may be changed in size, state or form,
the total mass cannot be changed. In other words,
these laws teach that no creation or destruction of mat-

ter or energy is now being accomplished anywhere in the physical universe.

The law of energy conservation is absolutely basic and of primary importance in all science. It was demonstrated quantitatively by scientists only a little over a century ago. However, the Bible has taught for thousands of years the same great truth that creation is no longer going on and that the present system is merely the finished result of an original divine creation. For example, Hebrews 4:3 affirms: ". . . the works were finished from the foundation of the world." Genesis 2:1, 2 says: "Thus, the heavens and the earth were finished, and all the host of them. And on the seventh day God ended his work which he had made."

This law of mass and energy conservation is also known as the first law of thermodynamics. It is the most important and basic law in all physical science.

The second law of thermodynamics, of almost as great significance, states the corollary law of energy deterioration. In any energy transfer or change, although the total amount of energy remains unchanged, the amount of usefulness and availability that the energy possesses is always decreased. This principle is also called the law of entropy increase, "entropy" being a sort of mathematical abstraction which is actually a measure of the nonavailability of the energy of a system.

Thus, in any closed system, regardless of how large or how small, the energy of the system must continually be degraded, as long as any energy change is taking place in the system—with some of the energy being dissipated in nonrecoverable friction or heat energy. Since all activities of nature (including biological activities) involve such energy transfers, there must be an ever-decreasing supply of usable energy for maintaining such processes in the universe as a whole.

This law of entropy increase is responsible for the fact that no machine can be constructed to 100 percent efficiency and that a perpetual motion machine is impossible. It is of primary importance in my own special fields of fluid mechanics and hydrology, and in all other disciplines of physical science as well.

Practically all the earth's energy, except its atomic energy, comes from the sun. However, by far the greater part of the tremendous amount of energy that the sun is continually radiating is dissipated into space in the form of unrecoverable heat energy. This prodigious waste of energy cannot last forever. Eventually, barring supernatural intervention, the sun must burn itself out, and then all activity on the earth must cease as well. The same principle applies to all the stars of the universe, so that the observable physical universe is, beyond question, growing old, wearing out, and running down.

But this law certainly testifies equally as well to the necessary truth that the universe had a definite beginning. If it is growing old, it must once have been young; if it is wearing out, it must once have been new; if it is running down, it must first have been "wound up." In short, this law of energy degeneration leads us to an affirmation of the necessary truth of the existence of a Creator, and a definite creation which took place in the past but which, according to the law of mass and energy conservation, is not continuing in the present.

Now let us note the teaching of Scripture concerning this principle of deterioration. For example, Psalm 102:25-27 says: "Of old hast thou laid the foundation of the earth; and the heavens are the work of thy hands. They shall perish, but thou shall endure; yea, *all of them shall wax old like a garment;* as a vesture shalt thou change them, and they shall be changed. But thou art the same, and thy years shall have no end." There are many other similar passages in the Bible. Thus, the Scripture teaches that which science has only discovered in the past hundred years.

However, the Bible also speaks often of that which science cannot discover: a future supernatural intervention of the Creator in his creation, destruction of the present system, and creation of "new heavens and a new earth," which "shall continue" and "wherein dwelleth righteousness" (Revelation 21:1; Isaiah 65:17; 66:22; II Peter 3:13).

Another truth indicated in Scripture is the basic equivalence of mass and energy. This was one of the most important discoveries of 20th century science. It is well known now that matter is actually one form of energy, a manifestation of atomic energy. The source of the tremendous energy of the atom is yet unknown and may be, in fact, unknowable by science. However, it is certain that a tremendous supply of power from some source is necessary to maintain the terrific motions and forces associated with the various sub-atomic particles. The magnitudes of such energies are graphically intimated in the energy released by atomic disintegration.

Most significant, then, is the proclamation of Hebrews 1:2, 3: "[God] hath in these last days spoken unto us by his Son, whom he hath appointed heir of all things, by whom also he made the worlds; Who, being the brightness of his glory, and the express image of his person, and *upholding all things by the word of his power,* when he had by himself purged our sins, sat down on the right hand of the Majesty on high."

This passage teaches that all *things*—that is, the matter of the physical universe—are maintained by energy or *power,* the source of which is the Creator himself, the Lord Jesus Christ!

The same tremendous truth is taught in Colossians 1:17, which is accurately translated thus in the Revised Standard Version: ". . .in him [Christ] all things *hold together.*"

Then in Hebrews 11:3 appears the following remarkably scientific statement: "Through faith we understand that the worlds were framed by the word of God, so that *things which are seen* were *not* made of *things which do appear.*" In other words, the matter of the universe is not ultimately physical, but is composed of something which is *not "apparent."*

All the mysterious nonphysical entities with which science deals—energy, electricity, magnetism, waves, gravity, and others—though intimately related to and associated with "things that are seen," are in themselves "things which do not appear." Much is known about their apparent behavior, but practically nothing about their ultimate character and source. Matter itself seems to be understandable only in terms of highly abstract mathematical "models" that bear little or no similarity to any of the large-scale physical phenomena with which we are familiar.

This situation would never have been admitted a few generations ago when scientists confidently felt that all things could be accurately and completely described in terms of the mechanical laws and models with which they were then familiar. Yet, once again, as scientific knowledge has increased, the Bible has been proven to be scientifically accurate.

There is another important inference from Hebrews 11:3 that should be mentioned. The forming of the "worlds" was not from pre-existing matter but directly by the Word of God!

We have now looked at a score of examples of modern scientific knowledge that were recorded in Scripture thousands of years before they were discovered by man. This ought to be abundantly convincing evidence of the supernatural source and inspiration of the Bible. But now let us examine briefly some of the most frequently cited examples of biblical error or contradiction.

"Where did Cain get his wife?" has long been a stock question among critics. The story of Cain, who was probably, although it is not definitely stated, the eldest son of Adam and Eve, is found in Genesis 4. As a result of his murder of Abel, Cain was condemned by God to be ". . . a fugitive and a vagabond." He went out to the land of Nod, east of Eden, where according to the 17th verse, ". . . Cain knew his wife; and she conceived, and bare Enoch: and he builded a city . . ."

This is commonly thought of as an inconsistency since—other than Adam and Eve—people have assumed that Cain was the only person alive at the time.

However, the Bible makes it clear, in Genesis 5:4, that Adam had other sons and daughters, and he lived to be 930 years old. The general rule of that day seemed to be longevity and prolificacy. In fact, the first command given Adam and Eve was to ". . . be fruitful and multiply." The ability to have children does not seem to have been affected by advancing age. It is stated that Noah, for example, was 500 old before he begat Shem, Ham, and Japheth.

If we accept the statement that men lived hundreds of years and continued to have sons and daughters most of their lives, then even using conservative birth rates it could easily have been possible for at least 20 million people to have been living on the earth at the time of Adam's death.

There would therefore have been plenty of women from which Cain could choose a wife and build many cities. Naturally in the beginning a son of Adam had to have married his sister. But there is no reason to assert that such a union would result in feeble-minded or deformed offspring. In those early days disease and the mutational effects of inbred heredity would not have begun to have the effect they have now.

Other questions, such as evolution and great length of life, will be considered in more detail later.

Another favorite target of most critics is the "fish story" of Jonah and the whale. It was formerly claimed that no whale possessed a gullet capable of admitting a man, to say nothing of the possibility of remaining in the belly of a whale for three days and three nights and living to tell about it. It is now known, however, that there are many varieties of whales with gullets large enough to easily admit objects much larger than a man. As a matter of fact, some have been found with whole sharks, three times the size of a man, in their stomachs. Furthermore, they have a habit of "vomiting out" the contents of their stomachs when dying, exactly as described in the story of Jonah.

The whale is not the only sea monster capable of swallowing a man alive. Harry Rimmer, in his book, *The Harmony of Science and Scripture,* tells of the amazing and well-authenticated case of a British sailor who was swallowed by a huge whale-shark and lived for two days and nights in his stomach. When the fish was caught the man was removed—unconscious but very much alive!

That Jonah's experience, even though we now know it could have happened under natural conditions, was nevertheless a miracle is attested to by the prophet himself. "The Lord had prepared a great fish to swallow up Jonah." And also, ". . . the Lord spake unto the fish and it vomited out Jonah upon the dry land." The story is further corroborated by Jesus Himself in Matthew 12:40, ". . . Jonah was three days and three nights in the whale's belly."

We shall consider one other case in this chapter—the long day of Joshua. In the great battle between the Israelites and the confederation of the Amorites in Joshua 10 it is related how ". . . the Lord fought for Israel" by two miracles: (1) causing the sun and moon to "stand still" in the midst of the heavens, "hasting not to go down about the space of a whole day," in order to give the children of Israel time to defeat the Amorites before nightfall; and (2) sending a great hailstorm, which probably served the twofold purpose of giving Joshua's army relief from the terrific heat and of slaying large numbers of the enemy. This storm was very likely a result of the atmospheric disturbances that would naturally result from the cessation of the earth's rotation.

Naturally, we have never observed any event of this sort. The Bible itself says that there was no day like that before it or after it. To say the story is untrue because it violates natural law is to imply that we know much more about such laws than we actually do. The reason for the earth's rotation upon its axis is itself a matter of pure conjecture; no one really understands why. The fact that it does rotate is a matter of observation, and since we've never observed anything else, we call it a "law."

But a law requires a "lawgiver," and it is the height of audacity to say that God could not suspend this law or invoke laws unknown to us if he so willed. There is no reason to suppose, furthermore, that a gradual slowing down of the earth's rotation would result in any profound geological disturbances. It *would* result in atmospheric disturbances, however. The same "law of gravity" that prevents our flying out into space, balancing the huge centrifugal force that is acting upon us as the earth whirls through space, would undoubtedly continue to act in such a way that all things in and on the earth would slow down simultaneously.

If this event actually took place, accomplished by a temporary slowing down of the rotational speed of the earth, it would be reasonable to suppose that people over the whole earth noticed it and made some record of it. These would now be preserved only in the form of semi-mythical recollections handed down in the folklore of these peoples, since written records of that period (about 1400 B.C.) have not survived, except in the Bible and in the fragmentary records of certain nations near the eastern shore of the Mediterranean.

It is significant, therefore, that intimations of such an event can be noted in the mythologies of many peoples from various parts of the earth. There are so many of them that they have even been used to bolster the theory that the biblical account was derived from them. In the book *Bible Myths* (Truth Seeker Co., 1882, p. 91), T. W. Doane describes accounts of a long day, similar to that of the Bible, in the Orphic hymns, in the legends of the Hindus, the Buddhists, the Chinese, the ancient Mexicans, and others. He draws the very dubious conclusion that the biblical record was therefore derived from stories such as these.

In the 1945 Report of the Smithsonian Institute, M. W. Stirling reported that one of the most persistent of the legends of the various American Indian tribes is that of the theft of the sun for a day. A similar legend is found among the Polynesians. The Greek legend of Phaethon, who disrupted the sun's course for a day, could easily have been derived from this event. Herodotus, the Greek historian, states that the priests of Egypt showed him records of such a day.

God has planned and maintained a very efficient universe which is normally subject to the operation of its regular laws. However, it is reasonable that, if his purposes were better served thereby, God would be expected on occasion to intervene in the normal operation of the "natural laws." Actually, these laws are upheld and maintained directly by the power of God.

The question in the case of any alleged miracle, is not whether it *could* happen, but whether it *did* happen. The question should certainly be decided in the affirmative if both of the following conditions are satisfied: (1) that there existed adequate reason, in line with his ultimate purposes, for God to intervene in the normally operative laws of nature; (2) that there exists adequate factual and testimonial evidence—such as would be used to prove any other historical event.

I believe that both these conditions are abundantly satisfied in all of the biblical miracles. With regard to Joshua's long day, there was certainly sufficient reason for God to perform such a miracle at this time. The success of Joshua's entire campaign depended on victory in this battle, and if he failed, the fulfillment of God's promises to the world through the nation Israel could not have been possible. Furthermore, the Canaanite peoples were sun worshipers, and it may well have been that God chose to accomplish their defeat through the instrumentality of their false god in order to unmask their exceedingly cruel and licentious religious system.

It should also be remembered that the miracle followed immediately after Joshua's command, uttered no doubt as a prayer of implicit faith. God promises even to remove mountains in answer to genuine faith.

As to the evidence for it, the very fact that the story appears in the Bible is itself strong evidence. As we shall see later, the historical portions of the Bible, including many phases of Joshua's conquests, have been substantiated in scores of instances by archaeological research. The Bible is now believed by nearly all authorities in Palestinian archaeology, including those who deny its supernatural inspiration, to be a highly accurate and reliable source of historical and geographical information.

Joshua (or perhaps a later copyist) was able also to appeal to a corroborative account of the miracle in the then-extant book of Jasher. We have already noted the existence of many semi-legendary recollections of such an event throughout the world. These alone are sufficient to establish the strong probability of the historicity of the biblical account.

The widely publicized theories of Dr. Immanuel Velikovsky should be mentioned here. Dr. Velikovsky and his followers believe that the earth has experienced a number of severe physical catastrophes caused by the entrance of a huge comet into the solar system. This comet eventually became the planet Venus. These disturbances lasted for several hundred years and according to Velikovsky's theory, caused many of the Old

Testament miracles such as the plagues of Egypt, the parting of the Red Sea, and the destruction of Sennacherib's army, as well as many prehistoric catastrophes recounted in the myths and legends of the world's early peoples.

The long day of Joshua is believed by Velikovsky to have resulted from a close encounter with the huge comet which disrupted and temporarily stopped the earth's rotation.

There is no need to enter into the details of these theories, which may be studied especially in his book *Worlds in Collision*. The theories have been rather vehemently opposed by most qualified physicists, astronomers, and geologists whose sciences would require revision should they be accepted. Undoubtedly many of their objections are quite legitimate but it nevertheless appears that his writings have had a definite and permanent impact upon science, if nothing else than to emphasize the dangers of a too-smug uniformitarianism which has characterized most geologic and astronomic theory for the past 150 years.

The Bible itself gives little direct support to Velikovsky's theory as a whole. The continual fire-and-brimstone type of environment in which the world's inhabitants would have had to have lived for hundreds of years certainly finds no corroboration in the matter-of-fact histories of the Old Testament. None of the miracles seem to harmonize in their details with the idea of a comet's approach.

Velikovsky's theories, true or not, have served to underscore the tremendous mass of accumulated evidence that very unusual events *have* taken place on the earth which cannot be explained by modern scientific dogma. He cites a great wealth of data from all over the world supporting the long day. This information can only be satisfactorily explained by the assumption that there actually was at one time a disruption in the earth's normal rotation which remains in the memories of tribes and nations all over the world.

We shall close this chapter with a very brief and inadequate mention of the most sacred and most profound doctrine of the Holy Scriptures—the doctrine of the Triune God. All true Christians believe in God the Father, God the Son, and God the Holy Spirit, and that these three, though distinct persons, are only one God.

Many, of course, do not understand this belief. It is contrary to established mathematical principles, they say, for Christians to maintain that $1 + 1 + 1 = 1$. It is unscientific and foolish, they are agreed, that the God of the universe, even though they should grant for the moment that he might be a real Personality, could be both one personality and three personalities at the same time. Therefore, it follows for them, that Jesus was not God in the biblical sense at all.

However, the doctrine of the Trinity is not only sound mathematically but is reflected in all true science in such a wonderful way that the assumed fact of an eternally existing Triune God is an inductive necessity before the universe can really be explained.

The doctrine of the Trinity is not set forth in the Bible as an explicit doctrine. But it appears indirectly as Jesus speaks of himself and of the Father and of the Holy Spirit. Always the order presented is: first, God the Father—the unseen Source and Cause of all things; second, God the Son—who tangibly and visibly reveals the Father to man and who executes the will of God; third, God the Holy Spirit—who is unseen and yet reveals God the Son to men through the media of other men and the Word which he inspired. This is not an order of importance or length of existence. All are equally eternal and equally God—one God. The Son is presented as "begotten of the Father," the Spirit as proceeding from the Father through the Son.

This triune relationship is clearly reflected in the physical universe. All knowable things in this universe may be classified under the heads of Space, Matter, or Time. Space, at least as far as we can comprehend it, consists of exactly three dimensions, each equally important and absolutely essential. There would be no space, no reality, if there were only two dimensions. Three distinct dimensions exist—yet each comprises the whole of space. To calculate the amount of any given space one does not add the length and breadth and width, but rather multiplies them together. Similarly, the mathematics of the Trinity is not $1 + 1 + 1 = 1$, but $1 \times 1 \times 1 = 1$.

The nature of Matter provides an even more striking analogy. The new physics has come to regard matter more and more as "simply" tremendous energy in motion. Depending on the rate and type of motion there are various phenomena presented to our senses— sound, color, heat, texture, hardness, and so on. Energy is the unseen source that manifests itself in motion and thereby produces some phenomenon. Matter involves these three phases and nothing that cannot rightly be included in one of these. Each is distinct yet each involves the whole of matter, and none of the three can exist by itself without the other two. Energy is first in logical, causal order, but not in order of importance or precedence. Motion, which embodies, reveals, and is begotten of energy, is the second. Phenomena proceed from motion and comprise the ways in which motion itself touches and affects men, even as the Holy Spirit reveals the Son and, through Him, the Father, to men.

Finally, Time is a third entity, but it consists of the future, the present, and the past. Each contains the whole of time, yet is distinct and cannot exist without the other two. The future is the unseen source of time and is embodied and made real, moment by moment, in the present. The past then proceeds from the present, becoming invisible again, yet continually influencing us. Finally, the great tri-universe itself consists of Space, manifested in Matter, and experienced through

Time, with each one of these three distinct entities pervading the whole.

Thus, every detail of the physical universe is remarkably cast in the same mold as that of the Triune God presented in the Bible. This cannot be coincidence. There must be an adequate cause for these resemblances.

But this same remarkable phenomenon can be seen in the realm of human life, as well. The Bible says that man was created in the image of God so this should be expected.

Each individual is a person who can be physically observed and described. Back of that person is his nature, which is unseen although it is the source of all that the person embodies. But that person, and through the person his nature, is known to other men only through his personality, which is an unseen, intangible thing. So, then, human life consists of three things—nature, person, and personality. They are equally important and equally the whole of the man, yet they always exist in the above logical order. None of the three can exist without the other two. Thus, man is, in minute detail, a finite reflection of God, who made him in his own image. It is true that sin has marred even this finite reflection but, nevertheless, man still reflects the image of God in an even more significant way than does the physical universe.

This same trinity seems to pervade everything in life. Every moral action of man consists of: first, the motive; second, the act; third, the consequences. The same relations apply among these as among the triunities we have already mentioned.

There seems to be a basic system of three-in-oneness pervading the whole creation. While these facts cannot be held to *prove* that the Creator of the universe and of life is a triune being, it is certainly difficult to formulate any other hypothesis as satisfactory as this to account for the existence of such universal triunity in nature. The doctrine of the Trinity is no unscientific, primitive absurdity, but intensely scientific and a tremendously important living reality. God was manifested and revealed by and in his Son, who as a man was Jesus Christ. There can be nothing more important for any individual, then, than to become rightly related to this triuniverse and its Triune God. This means unreserved acceptance of Christ, for "in him dwelleth all the fullness of the Godhead bodily."

The greatest scientists of all time—those who have laid the foundations of discovery and investigation that have contributed the most to all that is really worthwhile in our modern civilization—have in most cases been sincere, humble Christians who believed in the Bible as the literally inspired Word of God. Heading the list is Sir Isaac Newton, acknowledged by all to be the greatest man of science that ever lived. In the realm of physics, there was Lord Kelvin and Clerk Maxwell, almost equal in stature to Newton. The fathers of modern biology and medicine, Louis Pasteur and Lord Lister, may be included. In astronomy, the outstanding names are Galileo, Kepler, and Copernicus and, in modern times, Sir William and Sir John Herschel, all Bible-believing scientists. Pascal, Faraday, Ramsay, Pupin, Dana, Linnaeus, Agassiz, Dawson, and a long list of others could be added.

The Creation Research Society, organized in 1963, has a membership of over 600 scientists, all of whom have advanced degrees in a field of natural science and who believe in the full inspiration and authority of the Bible and the literal accuracy of the Genesis record of special creation. Though such scientists are still in the minority, their number is rapidly increasing. When I wrote the first edition of this book in 1945, it was almost impossible to find any advanced-degree scientists anywhere who were born-again Christians and creationists. Now there are thousands!

THE THEORY
OF EVOLUTION

3

Since the appearance of Darwin's famed *Origin of Species* in 1859, hundreds of volumes have been written on the evolutionary hypothesis by scientists, philosophers and theologians from every part of the world. At one time, the subject involved probably the greatest controversy in the scientific and religious realms since the time of Galileo. Eventually, however, the greater part of "Christendom" accepted evolution as a proven fact of science.

This theory is taught now as a fact in almost all the colleges and universities of the land. There is no longer any need, it is believed, to present proof of evolution or to argue the merits of the evolutionary interpretation. Students are supposed to take the fact of evolution for granted and to interpret everything else in the light of this one universal process. For the past 50 years the controversy has centered on how evolution works and what causes it.

Most of the churches and seminaries have occupied

themselves in revising their theology to fit the "advances" of science, a revision which was also deemed necessary in view of the work of the German "higher critics" who shrouded in doubt the authenticity and historicity of the biblical books.

It is a serious mistake to ignore, as many Christians seem to do, the tremendous implications and influence of the theory of evolution. By far the majority of college-trained men and women have been taught to accept evolution as a demonstrated fact of science, and it is now being taught almost universally in the high schools and even the grade schools of the United States. Evolution has, I believe, contributed more to the prevalent secularistic and materialistic philosophy of the world today than any other one influence. On the other hand, very few people have actually had the opportunity to study the great mass of evidence against the theory. Most are quite ignorant of the fact that very powerful contrary scientific evidence does exist.

There have been many theories widely held by scientists in the past which later had to be discarded. Many of the greatest scientific discoveries were at first powerfully opposed by established science. The fact that most scientists today believe in evolution is not in itself sufficient to prove that the theory is right. Science is continually changing. No textbook of physical or biological science writen 20 years ago could be used in a classroom today.

Evolution is not so much a science as it is a philosophy or an attitude of mind. Evolutionists agree that evolution requires aeons of time in which to work and that the few thousand years of written records available to us do not reveal one real example of genuine evolution taking place. Since no one was present to watch the alleged great evolutionary changes of the past, it is manifestly impossible to prove scientifically that they actually did take place.

In view of the rather speculative scientific ground on

which the theory stands, it seems hazardous to deliberately reject what God has revealed in the Bible about the origin of life in favor of an unproved hypothesis. Make no mistake: it is not possible to believe in both evolution and the Bible.

One does not need to read very far into the Bible before he sees very striking discrepancies between the two. Only by the most extreme distortion of the meaning of its words and statements can the account of the creation in Genesis be made to agree with the development of life presented to us by evolutionary geologists. Evolutionary geology supposes that living organisms originated in the sea countless millions of years before plants or any other forms of life appeared on the land. Genesis, however, states clearly that grasses, seed-bearing herbs, and fruit trees were created on the third day, and that sea animals (as well as land animals and birds) were not brought into existence until the fifth day.

Some have made much of the fact that the Hebrew word translated "day" may sometimes be used to indicate a long, indefinite period of time. This is true, but it is also true that in the overwhelming majority of cases it refers to a 24-hour period. Wherever it is used with an ordinal ("first," "second," et cetera) as it is here, it always refers to a 24-hour day. The great lights for ruling the day and the night were not made until the fourth day. It would certainly be quite lethal to the vegetation created on the third day if these days were longer than 24 hours. The use of the words "evening" and "morning" to describe the beginning and end of each day certainly would imply ordinary days as we know them.

Another problem with the day-age idea is that the Bible says death entered the world as a result of the sin of the first man and woman. However, if these days can be taken as long ages, then the bones of millions of God's creatures were buried in the ground before man was even on the scene. With such evidence of death and suffering prevailing throughout the world, it is passing strange that God would have pronounced his completed creation "very good" as he is said to have done in the last verse of Genesis 1.

Finally, God instituted the Sabbath as a memorial of his completed work. As far back as any records go mankind has been observing every seventh day as a day of rest. This is hard to explain unless God did actually rest after his work on the seventh literal day of creation. In Exodus 20:11, after incorporating the observance of the Sabbath into the law of Israel, it says: "For in *six days* the Lord made heaven and earth, the sea, and *all that in them is,* and rested the seventh day: wherefore the Lord blessed the sabbath day, and hallowed it." This command seems completely without force or meaning if the basis of the literal seventh day rest commanded by God was not his own literal seventh day rest.

If one regards the story of the creation as a beautiful but unhistorical allegory, striking difficulties appear in later parts of the Bible. Time and again throughout the Old Testament reference is made by the various writers to the Genesis story, always with the obvious belief on the writer's part that he is speaking of definite historical characters and events.

This is true in the New Testament, too. Paul refers again and again to the creation and fall of man. In fact, the fall of Adam and the resultant entrance of sin into the world is one of the basic doctrines of Christian theology presented by Paul. He drives home the fact that all men are sinners by nature because of the sin of the first man, Adam, and that it is only through the last Adam, Jesus Christ, that man can be freed from the penalties and consequences of sin (Romans 5:12-19).

Evolution, on the other hand, does not concede that man ever fell, but maintains that he has gradually risen from the state of the beast and is getting better all the time. Any evil that is in him is not sin inherited from Adam, but a holdover from his simian ancestors.

Even Jesus Christ believed in the Genesis record of creation. In Matthew 19:3-6, we read: "The Pharisees also came unto him, tempting him, and saying unto him, Is it lawful for a man to put away his wife for every cause? And he answered and said unto them, Have ye not read, that he which made them at the beginning made them male and female, and said, For this cause shall a man leave father and mother, and shall cleave to his wife: and they twain shall be one flesh?. . .What therefore God hath joined together, let not man put asunder."

Certainly, if Jesus really was the Son of God, as he claimed to be, he would not have based his teaching about such an important institution as marriage on a mythical or legendary event.

It is thus absolutely impossible to believe in the Bible as the complete and literal Word of God and to believe in the theory of evolution. But, more than that, it is quite irrational (as Sir Julian Huxley frequently emphasized) to believe in a personal God of any sort if one believes in evolution. Theistic evolutionists, who manage to think of evolution as "God's method of creation" are being inexcusably inconsistent. Evolution, by its very nature, is materialistic; it is nothing but an attempt to explain the facts of biology without the necessity of recourse to the supernatural or the divine. Mechanism and the doctrine of chance constitute the very quintessence of evolution.

If God actually did create the universe by the method of evolution then he appears to have selected the most inefficient and cruel and foolish method of doing it. If his goal were the creation of man, what possible reason could there have been for such misfits as dinosaurs to rule and roam the earth for millions of years, only to die out long before man arrived on the scene?

Evolution is supposed to have come about by means of the struggle for existence and the survival of the fittest. If true, this would mean that God deliberately instituted a law whose enforcement relied on the credo that might is right and the strong should exterminate the weak. Millions of animals must have perished in the course of the evolutionary process for no conceivable reason if, as the modernists assert, man was the ultimate goal. As one atheist professor put it: "The whole history of evolution reveals and witnesses that there is no intelligence back of the process. You cannot understand evolution and believe in God."

The atheistic and satanic character of the doctrine is evident in the many evil social doctrines it has spawned. Nietzsche and Marx, both radically atheistic, were profoundly influenced by the Darwinian ideas of natural selection and the survival of the fittest. They carried into the social and philosophic realms what Darwin and other evolutionists had attempted to apply to the biological realm. From Marx the world has inherited socialism, Communism, and anarchism. Nietzsche's philosophy profoundly influenced German political thought and became the basis of the intense German militarism of the first half of the 20th century. Mussolini was a most zealous disciple of Nietzsche and Fascism was the result. Nazism was bred in the same cesspool.

Evolution is also the basis of the many immoral doctrines taught in the psychological fields by Freud, Watson, Russell, Skinner and others. The gospels of gloom known as determinism and behaviorism have the same foundation.

It seems unthinkable that a theory of any kind could have had such far-reaching and deadly effects as has the theory of evolution. The very presence of goodness and beauty in the world makes it hard to believe such a theory could really be true.

Still, you may say, if science has proven that it is

true then we shall have to accept it regardless of the implications. That may be so, but we should certainly demand the most rigid and unquestionable proof before accepting such a harsh theory as proven fact. The purpose of this chapter is to make a brief survey of the alleged proofs that have thus far been offered by the evolutionists.

Evolution, as generally defined, means the gradual development of higher forms of life from simpler or lower types. The theory postulates a beginning which consisted of a single living cell that arose by spontaneous generation from a fortuitous combination of inanimate matter. From this cell evolved plants and multi-celled invertebrates, then fishes and insects, then amphibians, then reptiles, then birds and mammals, and finally man.

There is, of course, an absolutely fatal flaw right at the very outset. That is the impossibility of accounting for the origin of life in the first place. To dismiss the difficulty with the simple statement that life "appeared" at some time in the past when "conditions" were just right is little better than dishonest. The popular notion of spontaneous generation persisted in one form or another down to within the past century until it was demolished by Pasteur, Tyndall, and others. The same applies to the current notion of abiogenesis, which is the gradual development of complex molecules from basic elements until they finally become replicating molecules. In spite of its wide acceptance by evolutionists, neither is this process going on anywhere in the present world.

The so-called simple cell is really not so simple after all. It is known now that a cell is really a very wonderful and complex mechanism consisting of several component parts. It even has the faculty of reproduction. When it grows large enough, it simply divides into two parts, all parts of the cell being divided equally at the same time. Thus, two complete cells are formed where only one existed before. It is really quite impossible to see how such a complex organism as this could possibly have arisen spontaneously from inorganic matter, regardless of the "conditions." It is about as reasonable as saying that a skyscraper arose spontaneously from a pile of bricks and scrap-iron.

Living organisms are now known to be structured around a remarkable system called the DNA molecule (deoxyribose nucleic acid), in which is "encoded" all the "information" necessary to direct the growth of the complete organism from the germ cell. Although the variational potential in the DNA molecule is very large, allowing a wide range of variation in any given type of plant or animal, it also serves to insure that such variation will be within the fixed limits represented in the genetic systems of the parents.

In spite of much laboratory experimentation, it has not yet been possible to synthesize DNA or any other kind of replicating system from elemental non-living components. The tremendous amount of specific ordered information in any kind of imaginary self-replicating system is so great that it is almost inconceivable that scientists could ever synthesize it, and even more inconceivable that it could ever happen by chance. All the books ever written do not have as many units of information on their pages as does the DNA molecule.

Not only does the theory fail to account for the origin of life, but it cannot even provide a satisfactory explanation of the method by which evolution works. A great many proposed explanations have been offered by a great many investigators and theorizers, but the mechanism of evolution remains as mysterious today as it was a hundred years ago. Many modern biologists frankly admit their ignorance on this most important phase of their theory.

The first important suggestion offered was Lamarck's theory of the transmissibility of characters acquired through the effects of the environment or other external influences. This theory has been utterly disproved—both by experiment and by the advance in genetic theory—so it need not detain us here.

It is certain, however, that evolution would not have so speedily and so completely gripped the popular fancy if it had not been for the seeming reasonableness of the inheritability of acquired characters. Herbert Spencer insisted that evolution absolutely necessitated this type of heredity and that, if it did not take place, there could be no evolution. Darwin, Huxley, Haeckel, and other early evolutionists held similar opinions. But by the time of Weissman's experiments and germ-layer theory, which did more than anything else to demolish the Lamarckian theory, evolution had been so firmly established in the minds and literature of geologists and biologists that there was no stopping it.

Much the same dictum of complete rejection could be pronounced upon the Darwinian theory of natural selection. According to Darwin, the endless varieties and individual differences that are observed to occur among different members of the same species make occasional individuals better fitted to survive in the struggle for existence. These individuals then persist and transmit these favorable characteristics to their descendants, while others less fortunate gradually are eliminated. Infinite accumulations of these favorable heritable variations are invoked to account for the gradual formation of all forms of life.

Plausible as all this may sound, however, more detailed studies and knowledge of the specific and germinal characters of plants and animals have made it clear that natural selection alone cannot account for the origin of species. In the first place, it cannot account for the origin of the very necessary variations. The Mendelian laws of heredity, which were apparently unknown to Darwin and the other founders of modern evolutionary philosophy, showed that all these chance variations followed definite, though frequently quite complicated, arithmetical laws. They showed that, except under very extraordinary circumstances not usually occurring in nature, all variation is within certain fixed limits. No heritable characteristic could appear in an individual that had not existed in one, at least, of his parents (that characteristic may have been "dormant" and not appearing in the parent or even in several generations of ancestors, but was nevertheless present germinally).

The countless experiments which have verified Mendel's laws have, in recent years, been further substantiated by increased knowledge of the character of living cells. It has long been known that all living cells contain the substance called protoplasm. Upon this fact was built the once-revered Continuity of Life theory, according to which the cells were the smallest component of life and were the same for all living creatures. This theory was, of course, one of the main pillars of the theory of evolution. It is now known that all cells are not the same, but are fundamentally and definitely different among the various kinds. Even in the same creature, the cells composing different parts of the body are clearly distinct.

Each cell contains a number of component parts besides protoplasm. From the standpoint of genetics and heredity, the most interesting parts of the cell are the chromosomes. These are known to be the carriers of heredity. Each chromosome is a thread-like structure, and there is a definite number of them in each cell of the creature. This is true regardless of the part of the body in which that cell is located.

The number of chromosomes in each cell depends entirely upon the kind of organism in which the cells are found; for example, human cells contain 46 chromosomes. However, the germ cells of each sexually reproducing species contain only half the normal number of chromosomes for the species, so that when the chromosomes of the male and female germ cells unite, a new cell will be formed that contains the correct number of chromosomes for the species.

In order to explain theoretically Mendel's laws of heredity, the gene theory has been developed. According to this theory, each chromosome is composed of a large number of entities called genes. Each gene is supposed to govern or control some characteristic or group of characteristics in the individual. Also, various combinations of genes may influence characteristics. Recombinations and shufflings of genes can thus theoretically be invoked to account mathematically for all the fixed and variable characters that are observed in members of a species. Note, however, that all heredity is carried by the chromosomes and genes of the germ cells, which are formed very early in the development of an embryo. Consequently, any change in the body the body cells through use, disuse, or any other environmental influence, could have no effect on the germ cells and would not therefore be heritable. That is why acquired characteristics cannot be inherited.

Modern genetic theory is almost as lethal to the Darwinian hypothesis as it is to the Lamarckian, because by it all of the small chance variations which are supposedly acted upon by natural selection to form new species are really nothing but new combinations of genetic factors which were already in the parents in the first place. Thus nothing new is added and variation is held within fixed limits. Variability tends to hover about a certain mean. This has proven, by experience in nature, to be the best for the particular species concerned. Thus, instead of tending to produce new species, natural selection really acts to preserve those already in existence.

Darwin once said that if any part of any creature could not be explained on the basis of a slow accumulation of small changes, preserved by natural selection, his whole theory would break down. But this very thing is true of a very large number of organs and all kinds of living creatures.

For example, the wings of birds are supposed to have evolved by slow growths between the slowly lengthening toes of now-extinct reptiles. Yet it is quite impossible to understand how the wing ever got started. If some sort of a membrane happened to appear between the toes of a reptile in an incipient form, it would have been of no use for flying in its undeveloped state, and furthermore would have been a handicap to the creature while running. Consequently, according to the law of natural selection, the creature would have been less well equipped to survive than its relatives and would have perished. Similarly, it is very difficult to see just what survival value an undeveloped eye or an incipient heart would have had. This is true of any organ one can think of. It is also true of the marvelous thing called instinct in such animals as the beaver and in the various insects, such as the bee, the ant, and the water-spider. The instincts of these creatures, which are very marvelous and absolutely essential to their survival, must have evolved very suddenly in fully developed form if at all, because otherwise the species would have perished.

Furthermore, natural selection seems to require an almost infinite number of transitional forms in the origin of new and higher kinds. But this is not borne out by the fossil record which always reveals only very distinct forms. There are very few intermediate forms between established genera found either in living creatures or in the fossils. There are practically none between the families and comparatively few even between the species, despite the fact that species, genera and families are strictly arbitrary taxonomic categories invented for the convenience of biologists in classifying organisms.

The mutation theory was largely developed by Hugo

DeVries, in his work on the evening primrose, and T. H. Morgan, experimenting with the fruit fly. These and other workers observed that a distinctly new characteristic would sometimes suddenly appear in an individual. This change was called a mutation and it was found that the new character was heritable and that it followed the Mendelian laws.

Mutations were attributed to actual changes in the chromosomes or genes of the germ cells and have now become the most popular means of explaining evolution. It is usually stated that when mutations occur they are then acted upon by natural selection and, if helpful in the struggle for existence, they will survive and gradually form a new species.

However, this theory has been rejected by a large number of biologists and geneticists. In the first place, a great many "mutations" have proven to be nothing but recessive Mendelian characters which suddenly appeared when the right parents happened to come together. Furthermore, true mutations occur comparatively rarely in nature and when they do occur they usually disappear. This is because all genuine mutations that have thus far been observed are of either a pathologic or a neutral character. Never does a true mutation seem to be in the least degree beneficial. Most of the laboratory mutations have been induced artificially by chemicals, heat, x-rays, ultra-violet rays, or other mutagenic factors. These mutations are almost always recessive when crossed back with the original type. That is another reason why they will not persist in nature.

When one considers the great odds against a mutation being either beneficial to the organism or able to survive—and then realizes that the formation of a new species would require not one mutation but thousands—it demands a most amazing credulity to believe that this is the method of evolution responsible for the tremendous number of species of plants and animals in the world today. Yet that is precisely what is taught as gospel truth in probably the majority of schools. Recently, some evolutionists have been advocating a very rapid evolution by giant mutations which produce new kinds almost instantaneously. Such an idea has no observational basis, of course, and amounts to the same thing as turning a frog into a prince by a magic wand!

The majority of scientists continue to believe in evolution largely because of the alleged external proofs. We need to consider here only the most important of these proofs—those that appear most often in textbooks. None of them are convincing and are strictly circumstantial evidence at best.

Comparative anatomy is cited as one example. The anatomical and physiological resemblances between different species are considered to be evidence of relationship. For example, the general structural similarity between man and the ape, or between any other two mammals for that matter, is cited as proof of kinship. As a matter of fact, however, the structural *differences* between organisms are of greater significance than the more or less superficial similarities. Similarity of structure could better be cited as evidence of a common plan of creation, modified in details to meet specific needs. That would be the logical thing to expect in special creation.

The skeletal framework of every vertebrate is a model of design, specially arranged to accommodate the creature using it. The marvelous efficiency and ingenious construction of the skeleton is of especial appeal to the engineer interested in structural designing. It is safe to say that no building or bridge or any other engineering structure ever built could compare in excellence of design to the structural framework of the lowliest animal. Since all mammals, as well as man, have somewhat the same physical functions, it is only natural that the equipment for those functions should be similar.

The old argument from vestigial organs is still occasionally used in textbooks. According to this idea, certain supposedly useless organs in man, such as the appendix, the ductless glands, the coccyx, and others, are vestiges of useful organs left over from man's former animal existence. At one time there were supposed to be 180 of these vestigial organs in man. However, as ignorance was replaced by knowledge, and the use of these so-called useless organs was discovered, the number rapidly dwindled. Today most knowledgeable evolutionists would not claim any. A useless organ in a creature would be a poor proof of evolution, anyway! They are probably the results of mutational changes which, as we have seen, are usually harmful.

Evolutionists often point to the recapitulation theory, which teaches that the embryonic development of any organism is a condensed recapitulation of the past evolutionary development of that organism. This theory, first vigorously promulgated by Haeckel, precipitated much embryologic study for the purpose of building up the phylogenies (evolutionary histories) of different creatures.

Further paleontologic, embryologic, and biochemical investigations have dealt so hardly with the theory, however, that it has been quite generally discarded as a useful tool in embryologic or geologic research. Comparisons of many ontogenies (embryonic developments) with their supposed corresponding phylogenies as indicated by expanding paleontologic data, have revealed innumerable omissions, additions, accelerations, retardations and oversteppings. Consequently, the theory is now regarded by serious embryologists as incorrect. Though they still often choose to regard embryonic development in an evolutionary perspective, there is no longer any justification for using it as "proof" of evolution.

In the very early stages of development, there are many similarities among embryos of different species or even of different families. All embryos start from a microscopic germ cell and of necessity must develop along similar lines for a time, so resemblances are only to be expected; they are not an indication of genetic relationship. After about a month each type of embryo is visually distinguishable from those of other creatures.

Even before this, at any time after conception, an examination of the embryo's cell-structure would of course unfailingly reveal its true character. Much evidence has been gathered by qualified scientists showing that *every* stage in the development of an embryo is *quite necessary to the most efficient development of that embryo*. This is true in the case of every embryo that has been studied. The marvelous embryonic growth of all living creatures actually offers abundant testimony to the existence of a great Designer. It does not in any way give countenance to theories of materialistic origin and development.

We should mention here that the two main things that are absolutely essential to the theory of evolution have never been observed by man. I refer to (1) abiogenesis and (2) the natural development of a new and better-equipped, more complex "kind" from an old and less well-fitted kind.

Countless experiments have been done in an attempt to produce living matter from non-living. Without exception all have failed. Where men, guided by intelligence and the experience of centuries, have utterly failed, evolutionists insist that blind chance succeeded some time in ages past. This assumption goes against all experience and reason to bolster a theory that is both unproved and unprovable.

Given life, however, the theory requires that new kinds, more complex and better adapted to living, must arise by purely natural means from simpler and lower forms. If modern cytological and genetic research prove anything at all this seems absolutely impossible. As would be expected, within the recorded history of mankind there is not one example of such a transformation occurring.

Textbooks occasionally cite examples of new species arising in nature. When examined more closely, these examples almost invariably fall into one of two categories: (1) A new variety of the same species that has adapted itself to a changed environment. This quality of quick adaptation to environment is a matter of observation and, to a religious man, is attributable only to the providence of God, though brought about through natural agencies. Natural selection may explain the preservation of these changed types but it cannot explain their origin. (2) Degeneration. The universal law of nature seems to be stability or degeneration rather than evolution.

It is well to observe at this point that the Bible does not teach the fixity of species, for the simple reason that no one knows just what a "species" is. There are few issues more controversial among biologists today than this matter of what constitutes a species. Certainly, by many definitions of the term, some new species have "evolved" since the original creation. Genetic research has proven conclusively that chromosome changes, gene mutations, and hybridization can produce and, in fact, have produced many distinctly new varieties, in both plants and animals. These varieties are sometimes considered new species, or even genera by taxonomists.

However, all evidence thus far in the genetic field seems to prove conclusively that these agencies of change cannot go beyond certain comparatively narrow limits and can very definitely not produce new "kinds." The Genesis account merely says that each created group was to produce "after its kind," with no clear indication as to what constitutes a "kind." The

implication is that different kinds would not be interfertile, for if they were, they would not be reproducing
after their respective kinds. Thus, the biblical account
leaves ample room for just such conditions of change
within the smaller groups and stability within the
larger groups as is indicated by modern research.

The only "kind" we can be sure of is man "kind," and
all evidence is conclusive that, while the different
races of men are freely interfertile, man cannot cross
with any other creature on the earth. As has been previously noted, there are very definite limits of crossing
between the groups that, in modern taxonomy, are
called genera, and seemingly no crosses among the
families.

Thus, it is possible that the original Genesis "kind"
may in some cases be as broad as what the modern
systematist calls a "family." But let it be stated again,
in no uncertain terms, that there is no evidence that
evolution ever has occurred or ever can occur across
the "kinds."

Finally, then, the only real factual data upon which
the evolutionary hypothesis rests are provided in the
fossil record, which we shall now examine briefly.

The statement is frequently made in textbooks that
the fossils, as found in the sedimentary rocks of the
world, always indicate evolution. In the lower strata,
only simple and unspecialized forms are found and as
the surface is approached, increasingly complex types
appear. The thickness of sedimentary strata is supposed to be about one hundred miles, which of course
argues a tremendous antiquity for the earth. Sedimentary strata has been divided into a great many divisions and subdivisions according to the forms of life
found therein. This is indeed a strong argument and, if
one takes the interpretations of the biologists and
geologists at face value, it practically amounts to proof
that evolution has occurred in the past. However,

when we go from generalities to details, the case is not nearly so convincing.

The geologic divisions are not by any means universal around the globe. They present innumerable anomalies and contradictions. Methods of figuring geologic time are so inaccurate as to be practically worthless and are strongly influenced by subjective considerations. All of this will be discussed more completely later.

However, even if we assume for the sake of argument that the geologic time scale is trustworthy, several facts appear which are convincing evidence against evolution: (1) Many, many kinds of organisms have remained essentially unchanged through all the alleged millions and millions of years of geologic time. Many are now known and it is certain that many more would be recognized if it were not for the habit paleontologists have of giving new names to all fossil species regardless of how closely they resemble living species. Among the creatures that have thus remained unchanged through all the course of evolutionary history are the very protozoa with which evolution is supposed to have begun! This is difficult to understand if evolution is the universal law of nature. (2) A great many modern organisms are very evidently degenerate, rather than higher, forms of those that are found as fossils. These would include practically all mammals—elephants, tigers, wolves, apes, lions, rhinos, hippos, bears, beavers, and sloths. It is also true of multitudes of plants, as well as insects, birds, fishes, amphibians and reptiles (compare the dinosaurs to our modern snakes and alligators). (3) All of the great phyla, orders, and classes, as well as most families, genera and even species, appear quite suddenly in the fossil record, with no preliminary or intermediate forms. This has long been a serious problem for those evolutionists not content with glibly attributing this to the incompleteness of the fossil record.

(4) There is absolutely no objective reason, as will be shown in the next chapter, to believe that all or most of the fossil forms could not have been living simultaneously instead of being spread out over millions of years.

It would be well, however, to consider a few of the more publicized paleontological proofs of evolution. These "proofs" sound most impressive to the average student. The famous case of the horse is, according to the evolutionists' own claims, the best proof evolution has.

At the very most, the horse pedigree shown in popular evolutionary textbooks only suggests evolution within the family. Eohippus was small, about the size of a fox, with four toes on the front foot and three on the hind. The modern horse, of course, has only one toe on each foot, with possible vestiges of others. There are other minor differences between eohippus and equus, which, however, are mainly adaptations resulting from their difference in size. Between these two genera are about a dozen others, existing as fossils. Some of these had the same toe arrangements as eohippus, some had three toes on each foot, and still others have the side toes reduced to splints as in the modern horse.

However, all these animals are said to have lived in the Tertiary, late in geologic time. They are found near the surface, in the relatively unconsolidated Tertiary deposits. The different forms are not found superimposed one over the other, but at widely separated localities and often continents apart. No gradual evolution from one to the other is evident, but only a series of sudden jumps at best.

There is no clue to the origin of eohippus, who was as highly developed, specialized, and fitted to his environment as is the modern horse. Furthermore, he may not have been related to the other horses at all. Eohippus was quite similar to the modern hyrax, a rabbit-like quadruped found in Africa and southwest Asia.

All things considered, it seems quite plausible that each of the several genera may have been living simultaneously. Perhaps they were mutant variants of the originally created horse kind which have, like many other zoological inhabitants of that former age, for one reason or another become extinct.

Even if one of these forms actually should prove to be the ancestor of the modern horse (and such has not yet been proven by any means) the loss of one or more toes could be attributed to a mutation. As with all known mutations this would be a deterioration rather than an advance. As for size, it is obvious that there are many families in the present world containing members differing in size quite as much as eohippus and equus. Some modern midget horses, in fact, are not significantly larger than eohippus. Furthermore, many fossil horses have been found, in many regions, which were as large and sometimes larger than the modern horse. Many of them seem, in fact, quite identical with equus, though others have three toes and other differences.

All things considered, this supposed best demonstration of evolution falls more than somewhat short of being such a demonstration at all. The same criticisms could be brought against the evolutionary pedigrees of the camel, the elephant, and other animals. Archaeopteryx, often described as a transitional form between birds and reptiles, is known to have had feathers, and thus to have been a true bird. Furthermore, recent finds of fossil birds older than archaeopteryx have proven that, whatever it was, it could not have been an evolutionary ancestor of the birds.

There remains, then, the problem of the fossils that have been classified as pre-human. Upon examination of these finds, which are extremely fragmentary and questionable, it becomes clear that they are very poor demonstrations of the theory of man's descent from the ape. Thousands of fossilized apes have been found, representing both living and extinct species. Similarly, a great many fossilized skeletons of modern man have been found, but most textbooks are strangely silent about that. Only a very few teeth or bone fragments exist which could be imagined into any sort of a lower species of man. The very paucity of such evidence is alone enough to demolish the theory of man's relationship to the ape.

When I was a college student (1935-39), I was taught that the main fossil proofs of human evolution were Java Man, Heidelberg Man, Piltdown Man, Neanderthal Man and Peking Man. None of these are considered very significant today. The most notorious is the famous Pithecanthropus Erectus, found in Java in 1891 and 1892. This find consisted of a part of a skullcap, a fragment of a left thigh-bone and three molar teeth.

These fragments were not found together but within a 50-foot range. They were discovered over the course of a year's work in an old river bed, far below the high water mark, mixed with debris and the bones of extinct animals.

The skullcap was pronounced by most paleontologists who examined it to be distinctly that of a large ape or gibbon. There was much debate over the teeth and thigh-bone: some said they belonged to an ape, some said human, others said ape-man. In later years, the Dutch scientist who discovered it, Dr. Dubois, reversed his opinion as to the missing-link character of his find and declared the skull and teeth to be the remains of some form of gibbon. Yet this was universally acclaimed by evolutionists as an outstanding proof of man's evolution.

In recent years there have been other finds in Java which have affected the status of Pithecanthropus. He is now regarded by most present-day anthropologists as essentially identical with man. The original skull has come to be regarded by some as that of a small woman. The femur is admittedly completely human in form. The teeth were probably simian and did not belong with the other remains at all. It is noteworthy that Dubois himself found, in the same deposits where Pithecanthropus was found, two other skulls. Each of them was completely human in all details. In 1936 a perfectly human jawbone and skullcap, belonging to an infant, were found in Java in a stratum *below* that of Pithecanthropus.

The well-known Heidelberg Man is supposed to be another pre-human. He consisted of a large jawbone found in Germany in 1907. The teeth are quite human and except for the receding chin (a feature which is common to quite a few moderns), the large jawbone had been found to be accurately duplicated in many Eskimo, Tasmanian, and New Caledonian skulls, none of which have the ape-like appearance that had been attributed to the Heidelberg Man.

The Piltdown Man of England was discovered over a period of several months and in an area of several square yards. It consisted of a few skull fragments, a tooth, and a piece of jawbone. This creature was reconstructed by several experts. Some gave him the skull of a human, some made him an ape, some made him an ape-man, and some were adamant that the different bones did not even belong to the same creature. Finally, the entire set of bones was proved to have been planted as a hoax! A great many of the evolutionists themselves have repudiated this find, which was for a long time nevertheless offered as proof in most textbooks.

The Neanderthal race of cavemen has been more widely publicized perhaps than any other of these ancient men, except possibly Pithecanthropus. The original Neanderthal Man consisted of a skullcap, described by various authorities as belonging to an ape-man, a negro, an idiot, a modern Cossack, an early German, and several other things. Since that time, a number of other skeletons and fragments have been found in Europe and other points around the Mediterranean. Many of these are questionable, but some evidently belonged to the Neanderthal Man which the great majority of paleontologists now say was identical in species to modern man. Frequently perfect Neanderthal types appear among modern peoples. It seems more probable that the Neanderthals represented a degenerate tribe, rather than a developing race.

The Peking Man is represented by quite a number of individual skulls found in caves near Peking, China. The first was found in 1929 and acclaimed as an important "missing link." Some authorities, however, believed them to be the skulls of monkeys. With the discovery of more remains at the Peking site, however, it was found that some of them were quite modern. Others were similar to the Neanderthal type. The original Peking Man fossils were lost during World War II and never adequately studied for their real nature.

There are others that might be discussed, but those already mentioned are the best known and were supposed to have provided the best evidence for human evolution. This whole subject seems replete with varying opinions and ever-changing interpretations on the part of the different experts involved.

The past 60 or so years have even witnessed a number of outright boners on the part of authorities. There was the Pithecanthropus skull, found in Java in 1926, that turned out to be an elephant's knee bone. Then there was the Hesperopithecus tooth found in 1922 in Nebraska. This was so widely accepted as proof of man's antiquity that it was introduced as evidence by the evolutionists during the famous "monkey trial" in Tennessee in 1925. Two years later, however, the complete skeleton was found and it proved to have belonged to an extinct pig. The so-called Colorado Man (also constructed from a tooth) was later found to have belonged to the horse family. An ape-man skull, also found in Colorado, was exhibited in a museum until it was found to be the skull of a pet monkey buried a few years previously. A bone found near Seattle and identified as an ancient human fibula turned out to be part of a bear's hind leg.

In recent years, interest has shifted to the many fossil forms discovered by Dr. Leakey and others in South Africa. Most are identified as Austrolopithecus. There has been a sharp difference of opinion among anthropologists as to whether or not the Australopithecines were part of the line of human evolution. The question has apparently been settled, however, by the discovery of several fossil forms clearly belonging to the genus *Homo* (true man). These have been dated much earlier than the Australopithecines.

The situation currently (1978) is that man is "older" than any of his so-called ancestors. Some anthropologists are even suggesting now that apes are the evolutionary descendants of man! In any case, all available evidence is compatible with the biblical teaching that men have always been men and apes have always been apes. It is even possible to explain some of the fossil men as from tribes that became isolated after the dispersion at the Tower of Babel and then, through inbreeding and harsh environmental conditions, deteriorated physically and finally became extinct.

These facts serve to add emphasis to the rule that developmental evolution is *not* the universal law of biology, but rather deterioration or degeneration. As we have seen, there is no real evidence of progressive evolution, but very much evidence for deteriorative evolution or, at best, biologic stability.

We have already seen that this law of degeneration, or entropy increase, is universally operative throughout the physical and chemical realms; it now seems also to pervade the biologic realm. In fact, this truth is beginning so to disturb evolutionists that several significant papers have appeared recently in scientific journals attempting to harmonize the concept of evolution with the second law of thermodynamics.

More and more it appears that there is one great degenerative principle pervading all nature, of which the law of entropy is merely its formal expression in physical phenomena. This has been called by Dr. R. E. D. Clarke the "law of morpholysis" (morpholysis means "loosing of structure"). In other words, there is a universal tendency from the highly organized to the disorganized, from the ordered to the disordered. Never is there an inherent, natural, undirected, unaided, trend toward increase of order or organization. The natural tendency is always downward.

In biology an important example is found in the very agencies supposed to bring about evolution, i.e., gene mutations and chromosome changes or aberrations. All such changes are harmful or at best indifferent, as far as the organism is concerned. They seem clearly to represent a breakdown of the original ordered arrangement of the genes in the germ cells, brought about through penetration of the germ cell by X-rays, cosmic radiation, or some other disorganizing medium. In some way the genetic structure is disarranged and since if the mutations are not actually lethal they are both harmful and hereditary, the eventual result is a deterioration of the racial stock.

This would most likely account for the fact that most of the living creatures of today are represented in the fossil record by larger, more highly developed forms of living creatures. It would, furthermore, explain the phenomenon of the atrophy of once-valuable organs until they become vestigial, or even disappear.

Evolutionists may still insist that the law of entropy does not preclude evolution since biological systems are open systems and can draw energy from the sun to support an upward evolution. The fact is, however, no one has ever seen any type of organism evolve into a more complex organism, while there are innumerable examples of harmful mutations, deteriorations and extinction.

Scientific generalizations should be based on observation, and all known examples of systems in which order increases for a time (e.g., growth of an organism, erection of a building) have a complex program available to direct the growth and an energy conversion mechanism available to convert the sun's energy into the specific work of growth in complexity. These factors enable such a system to overcome its innate tendency toward disorder. The supposed evolutionary progress of the biosphere, however, has no such directing code or conversion mechanism available to it.

Thus, it seems evident that if evolution has taken place on any large scale at all (that is, of course, progressive evolution) it must have done so at complete variance with the indications of all modern genetic research and indeed with all basic physical law. Most of the evidences for evolution can be better interpreted in the light of the law of deterioration, and with far better scientific basis.

MODERN SCIENCE
AND THE FLOOD

4

In the book of Genesis, beginning at the sixth chapter, we have the record of what seems to have been the greatest catastrophe this earth has experienced since man first appeared. All men, as well as all land animals, except those whom God chose to save in the ark, were destroyed by a great world-enveloping Flood.

The biblical record of the deluge clearly refers to a great world-wide Flood. Some writers, because of alleged geological and archaeological difficulties, have maintained that the Flood was only a localized catastrophe, applicable at most only to the known world of that time. Most critics of the Bible have, in fact, dismissed the entire tale as purely legendary.

However, if the Bible is allowed to speak for itself, an open-minded reader would surely understand the writer of the account to be referring to a worldwide deluge. Consider the following passages, which can be sensibly understood in no other way:

Genesis 6:17, "I do bring a flood of waters upon the

earth, to destroy all flesh, wherein is the breath of life, from under heaven; and every thing that is in the earth shall die."

Genesis 7:4, "Every living substance that I have made will I destroy from off the face of the earth."

Genesis 7:19, 20, "And the waters prevailed exceedingly upon the earth; and all the high hills, that were under the whole heaven, were covered. Fifteen cubits upward did the waters prevail; and the mountains were covered."

Genesis 7:23, "And every living substance was destroyed which was upon the face of the ground, both man, and cattle, and the creeping things, and the fowl of the heaven; and they were destroyed from the earth: and Noah only remained alive, and they that were with him in the ark."

Genesis 9:11, "And I will establish my covenant with you; neither shall all flesh be cut off any more by the waters of a flood; neither shall there any more be a flood to destroy the earth."

One or two such passages might be passed off as figurative or as examples of Hebrew literary exaggeration, but when the same theme of universal inundation and destruction is emphasized again and again and again it seems quite unreasonable to attempt to impress any other meaning upon the account.

It is quite likely that with the conditions of longevity described in the Bible, the earth's population would have so increased by this time (more than 1,600 years after the creation of Adam) that a large part of the earth would almost certainly have been populated. Therefore a worldwide Flood would have been necessary if all mankind were to be destroyed.

If all the mountains in the immediate vicinity—including the mountains of Ararat, one peak of which is over three miles above sea level—were submerged, it would quite obviously be impossible for the Flood *not* to have also attained the same elevation in other regions. The record states that such conditions prevailed for 150 days at least.

But even more importantly, the entire story is absurd if the Flood described is only a local flood. The elaborate provisions for the preservation of life in the ark were utterly unnecessary. God could merely have warned Noah to move to another region rather than to build the ark. The same is true for the animals, which the record says God caused to come to the ark; the birds especially might easily have flown to dry land.

The biblical record implies that the cause of the Flood was both tectonic and atmospheric. Such a gigantic catastrophe must have profoundly changed the geographic and stratigraphic features of the earth's surface as it was then. This would make it impossible now for men to discern with any degree of assurance any geologic activity that had taken place in the years before the Flood. Thus, if there actually was a worldwide aqueous calamity of the sort described in the Bible, the fossil record becomes meaningless, so far as evolution is concerned. As we have seen, world history as interpreted from fossils is the only evidence of any value remaining for the theory of evolution. Consequently, in spite of overwhelming ethnological, philological, archaeological, and geological evidence that there actually was a universal deluge, evolutionary scientists dogmatically maintain that the Flood story of the Bible is purely legendary.

The credo which has been held by most geologists for nearly a hundred years is called uniformitarianism. This doctrine "assumes the assumption" that the origin and development of all natural, observable phenomena, in both the living and nonliving realms, can be explained by natural laws and processes operating essentially as they do today.

As applied to geology, it means that all the mountains, the rivers, the huge stratigraphic deposits—in short all features of the earth's surface—are the result of the slow processes of sedimentation, erosion, contraction, radioactivity, and other actions of natural forces, all working over almost infinitely long periods of time. This theory is based not on objective proof but on a process of rationalization. It is considered unscientific to invoke unnatural events such as creation or the Flood to explain phenomena that now seem to conform to natural laws and uniform processes.

The popularity of uniformitarianism dates from its enunciation by Sir Charles Lyell, whose theories profoundly influenced the work of Charles Darwin. However, the idea was not new; its origin is hidden in the obscurity of antiquity and has always found expression in some form or other. With the renewed interest in both science and Christianity during the Renaissance period, nevertheless, the dominant theory of geology became the Flood theory and remained so until the time of Lyell and Darwin.

A great many brilliant investigators believed the Flood theory, not because of personal philosophy or faith, but because of thousands of observed facts in the field. It is true that some of these early geologists developed bizarre explanations for some of the data, but the common-sense logic of many of their writings is still irrefutable.

The geologic time scale, which we mentioned previously, is the backbone of the uniformitarian view of geology. It was worked out long ago, chiefly from the observed order of the fossils in a small corner of western Europe and in New York State.

There are assumed to have been four great eras. The Primary, which includes the Archaeozoic and the Proterozoic eras, is supposed to represent the ages before life appeared to any extent on the earth. It is characterized by those rocks which contain few or no fossils. These are supposed to be the oldest rocks of all.

The Paleozoic Era is marked by rocks containing fossils of the lower forms of life, especially invertebrates, fishes, insects, and amphibians. It is subdivided into several large systems according to the forms of life found in the various rocks. These systems are— beginning with the oldest—the Cambrian, the Ordovician, the Silurian, the Devonian, the Mississippian, the Pennsylvanian, and the Permian. Further subdivisions exist in each system.

The Mesozoic Era is supposed to be the age of reptiles and is divided into the Triassic, the Jurassic, and the Cretaceous.

The Cenozoic Era is the last of the geologic eras and is divided into two main systems. The first of these is called the Tertiary and is also known as the age of mammals. There are five series in this system known, in ascending order, as the Paleocene, the Eocene, the Oligocene, the Miocene, and the Pliocene. The other system is usually called the Quaternary and includes the Pleistocene Series, in which man is supposed to have appeared (although many paleontologists now claim that man must have appeared well back into the Tertiary. The skeletons and artifacts of true humans have been found in Tertiary deposits). The Quarternary also includes the Recent, often called the age of man.

It is usually taught in textbooks that this order is inviolable and is observed all over the world. This idea, in a different form, was first developed by Professor Werner, a German who taught that the stratigraphic deposits always occurred in the same vertical order according to their mineral or lithologic character— granites, limestones, schists, sandstones, et cetera. This theory was called the "onion-coat" theory and was very widely held by materialistic geologists for a long time. It has now given way to a theory of biological onion-coats, in which the order of the fossils is thought to be always the same. The mineral or lithologic nature of the rocks is now considered immaterial, the age and chronological position of any given formation depending solely upon the contained fossils.

The circle of reasoning involved here should be immediately evident. The fact of evolution is necessarily assumed in building up the geological series; rocks containing simpler fossils are called old, and rocks containing more complex and specialized forms are considered young. Then the paleontological series thus constructed is taken as proof of the fact of evolution.

This method of identifying the rocks cannot be overemphasized. The physical characteristics and even the stratigraphical position are given only very minor consideration when their age is being decided. This decision depends almost entirely upon the contained fossils and is usually settled by laboratory workers who may never have seen the actual deposits.

However, in spite of the apparent circular reasoning involved in such procedures, this system of classification seems to have worked out fairly satisfactorily in North America and Europe. There still remains considerable doubt as to its ultimate correlation with the geology of other parts of the world. It seems that, in general, the time-order of deposition of the strata is represented fairly well by the geologic time-classification as given. The really essential point of difference between the commonly accepted geology and Flood geology is not the *relative time* of deposition of different rock strata, but the actual *total time* elapsed while they were being deposited.

The accepted stratigraphic order and system is far from inviolable and involves many hard-to-explain exceptions and anomalies. In the first place, the total depth of all fossiliferous strata is supposed to be over 100 miles. However, the greatest depth ever measured is about 15 miles and the average only about one mile. In any one exposure, two or three systems or even fewer are all that are usually represented. At no place in the world does the complete or even partially complete geological column exist. The theory has been built up entirely by the superposition of deposits from all over the world.

Furthermore, very many different formations, widely separated in geologic time, have been found resting directly upon the Primitive rocks. Many cases have been observed here in America of the very youngest Quaternary rocks resting directly upon the Primary with all the intervening ages omitted. The same thing can probably be said for every rock system of importance. The very oldest rocks (i.e., non-fossil-bearing) may be on the surface and have the physical appearance of young rocks, soft and unconsolidated. Young rocks, on the other hand, may well be as indurated or even metamorphic as the very oldest.

It is also generally accepted in geology that any fossiliferous formation may lie directly upon any other formation in the whole of the series below it, and that it is not at all to be expected that a given formation need lie directly upon the formation that immediately precedes it in geologic age. When intervening formations are missing, it is assumed that the missing periods can be accounted for as periods of erosion rather than deposition. Often, however, the missing periods are not at all obvious physically, and are only inferred from fossil evidence. They are called disconformities or diastems when the beds on both sides seem to have been normally deposited without intervening deformation. Quite often the two sets of beds are parallel and give every indication of having been deposited successively without any great period of time or erosion between. The disconformities are, in such cases, discernible only on the basis of the contained fossils.

If it were not for the preconceived opinions about the evolutionary sequences of the fossils, there would be no reason for saying that such beds could not have been deposited with no great lapse of time between. This sort of thing is not an isolated phenomenon, but occurs quite frequently.

Even more surprisingly, many cases are known to geologists of strata occurring in the wrong order and, furthermore, in perfect conformity. That is, great areas containing "old" fossils are found to rest perfectly naturally upon rocks containing "young" fossils. Sometimes such inversions have obviously been produced by normal faulting and folding, of which the rocks of the earth's crust give much evidence. Often, however, there is no physical indication at all that the beds came to be in their existing positions by any other means than normal deposition. This cannot be allowed, however, because it would immediately prove that the "young" fossils are older than the "old" ones, at least in time of deposition, and this would obviously necessitate sacrificing the notion of organic evolution.

To avoid such conflict, we have the remarkable theory of the horizontal thrust fault. According to this theory, great masses of rock were severed from their original formations, and somehow lifted up and shoved over on top of the adjacent areas. Afterwards, surface erosion through subsequent ages removed the upper deposits, finally leaving only the older rocks lying on the younger ones beneath!

If such things as this have ever happened upon the planet, they must have been caused by forces of far greater intensity than anything ever observed by humankind in the present age. There is most certainly no experimental or observational basis for such an explanation. This fact in itself is most inconsistent with the geologic dogma of uniformity. No less an authority than Wm. Bowie, long-time Director of the U. S. Coast and Geodetic Survey, and one of the world's greatest authorities on isostasy and tectonics, called horizontal faulting "absurd, from an engineering point of view."

Nevertheless, scores of examples of this phenomenon exist. Every large mountain range in the world that has been adequately examined (and mountainous regions are the ones that *have* been most thoroughly examined geologically) has been found to contain large areas of these upside-down strata.

A vast area in Montana and Alberta, including all of the Glacier National Park, has fossils of the Paleozoic Era and earlier overlying formations containing dinosaur bones and other fossils of the Cretaceous. This region is the divide between not only the Atlantic and Pacific Oceans, but also between Hudson Bay and the Gulf of Mexico. Thus, the very highest region of North America consists of a stratum of Pre-Cambrian limestone resting perfectly naturally (at least at many exposures) on a Cretaceous bed.

In Tennessee and Georgia, a great "fault" continuing for hundreds of miles consists of Cambrian deposits resting quite normally on Carboniferous.

The great Bannock Overthrust of Utah and the Heart Mountain Thrust of Wyoming, along with many other examples in the Rockies, offer more illustrations of huge areas of rocks, thousands of feet thick, that must have been shoved up and over the adjacent areas, without leaving adequate evidence anywhere of their incredible journeys. Much of the Swiss Alpine region is in this upside-down condition. The same is true of the Scottish Highlands and the mountains of India. One of these displacements in northern China has been followed for more than five hundred miles. A similar area of some 85,000 square miles is known in Scandinavia. Every part of the world yields other examples.

However, even if the geologic time-scale is assumed to be substantially correct as far as the relative positions of the various strata are concerned, the Flood theory can account for their deposition as satisfactorily as the theory of great ages.

The pre-deluge world, like the present world, was undoubtedly one in which lived a great variety of different kinds of creatures. Then, as now, they did not all live together or in the same type of environment, but each particular kind lived in an environment for which it was fitted.

Therefore, a great cataclysm of the kind described in the Bible would not be expected to pile all types of creatures together heterogeneously throughout the world. Rather, it would necessarily destroy together the particular assemblages of creatures living in the same environment. The currents would bring such assemblages together, and finally bury them together. This, of course, could not be expected to be an inviolable rule, but it would generally hold true. Thus, two or more strata might be deposited quite simultaneously, but contain completely different groups of future fossils, because of their different sources, directions of transport and final deposition localities.

On the other hand, evolutionary geology teaches, by implication at least, that only one assemblage of organisms was living at any one time in the history of the world and that, therefore, these organisms can be used to identify any rock strata formed during that age. There can be no basis for this assumption other than evolutionary presuppositions, because such is certainly not the case in the modern world, which is supposed to be "the key to the past."

The biblical deluge was both terrestrial and atmospheric in nature. Tremendous volumes of water poured from the heavens for 40 days and nights. At the same time, the "fountains of the great deep were broken up." This implies great subterranean and subaqueous disturbances which would have created great tsunami waves and ejected great amounts of juvenile water. The great complex of hydrodynamic currents and forces thus generated would then undertake its divinely ordained mission of destruction and purification of the antediluvian world.

Such a Flood would necessarily tend to affect first the creatures inhabiting the deep ocean, followed by those

in shallower waters. Then the waters and disturbed
sediments would overtake the amphibious and coastal
creatures. Above these would be buried swamp, marsh,
and low river-flat creatures, including reptiles. Higher
mammals would usually be able to retreat from the
rising waters to some extent, but also would be eventually drowned and perhaps buried in the sediments.
Finally man, the chief object of the waters, would be
overtaken and carried under. Thus the Flood would in
general have tended to form strata in the order the
geologic age scale places it. These strata would
perhaps in many instances have been reworked and
redeposited by retreating flood waters, and perhaps
also during the succeeding centuries.

In its semi-plastic state during and right after the
Flood, the land would have been subject to much distortion by the great forces generated by the hydrostatic
and hydrodynamic pressures of the deluge waters, and
by the redisposition of the prediluvian topography.
This might partially account for the existence of the
great faults and folds in the sedimentary rocks of the
crust.

Another factor affecting the deposition of the strata
would be the sorting action of moving water, which
would tend to separate organic and inorganic particles
into assemblages of similar sizes and shapes. The
speed at which particular fossils settled and were deposited would be at least partially controlled by their
specific gravity, size and shape. The more dense
marine organisms would therefore tend to settle first,
then amphibia, mammals, et cetera. Within a given
formation, the simpler, more streamlined organisms
within a given kind would tend to settle out lower than
the more complex individuals of that kind.

This, of course, is but the barest outline of the probable geologic activity caused by the deluge. Further
geologic work would be accomplished on the surface as
the land was uplifted in places and the waters re-

treated. Abnormal geologic and meteorologic conditions perhaps prevailed for centuries before the present condition of approximate equilibrium in the earth's crust and atmosphere was attained. The tremendous release of energy at the Flood might even cause rupture and spreading-apart of the continental areas originally uplifted after the Flood.

The deluge theory, then, seems to offer an acceptable framework within which to explain all the multitudinous data with which geology deals. The main criticism of the theory has always been on the basis of the time element involved. It has been maintained, by those few geologists who have adequately considered it and then rejected it, that the immense sedimentary rock beds of the earth and their fossils cannot possibly be attributed only to one great cataclysm, but that their formation must have occupied aeons of time. This assertion cannot be proved, however, in the very nature of the case.

Obviously, in a book of this sort, it is impossible to have a thorough discussion of all phases of geology, and show how the various phenomena and formations harmonize with the Flood theory. However, most of these problems are dealt with in the books listed at the end of this book. In spite of the fact that there have been thousands of uniformitarian geologists over the past century and only a few creationist geologists to reinterpret the accumulated volumes of data, the Flood model will be seen to encounter far less serious scientific objections than the presently accepted uniformitarian model.

As a matter of fact, the Flood theory of geology is very little if any less uniformitarian in character than orthodox geology. The catchword of the uniformitarian view of geology is that "the present is the key to the past." However, one does not go very far in the study of historical geology, as now interpreted, before he sees that "uniformitarianism" is actually a rather gross misnomer. Present geologic processes, such as erosion, sedimentation, volcanism, diastrophism, glaciation, and others are supposed to be able to account for all stratigraphic and physiographic phenomena. However, if the current rate of activity among these agencies is to be considered typical of what went on in the past, it is obvious that they could not have begun to accomplish the things they did.

In recent years, in fact, many geologists have recognized the limitations of the kind of consistent uniformitarianism that has been advocated by practically all geologists since the time of Lyell. They have come to recognize the necessity of a rather large extrapolation from present geologic processes in order to make a reasonable accounting for the existence of many of the earth's geologic phenomena.

For example, when in recorded history has there ever been a great outpouring of volcanic lava such as must have formed the terrain that extends over great areas of the Pacific Northwest and many other parts of the world? Where has there ever been observed a mountain uplifted thousands of feet against the huge forces of gravity and friction? What about the great rock ruptures that are supposed to have formed the Great Rift of Africa, the formation of the great fault-scarp on the eastern edge of the Sierra Nevadas, or the one that formed the Grand Tetons, or thousands of others almost as spectacular?

Speculative geologic history is replete with the erosion of vast peneplains, but where is such to be found in the modern world? Wherein lies the present-day observational basis to account, on the basis of uniformity, for the great ice-sheets, thousands of feet thick, that are supposed to have covered most of Europe and North America many times in past ages? What about the coal beds, which are said to have been formed over long ages as the result of alternate submergences and emergences of peat bogs, the cycle repeated scores of times on the same spot (and this in spite of the fact that many fossil tree trunks have been found extending through several coal seams, each presumably formed during one such cycle)?

Who has actually observed great canyons excavated through solid rock to depths of thousands of feet? Or the deposition of great silt deposits over great areas and hundreds of feet deep by peri-glacial winds? Or the formation of great alluvial plains hundreds of square miles in area and hundreds of feet deep? What modern river has been responsible for any of these things? Such events as these, and very many more with which historical geology deals, most definitely cannot be adequately described or explained in terms of their modern counterparts.

Even the customary appeal to great ages of time cannot be made in many such instances. Modern volcanoes could never produce the volcanic terrains seen in many parts of the world. Man has never observed the tremendous igneous intrusions responsible for forming the great dikes and sills, the great batholiths, and other igneous formations. The slight earth movements of our era, even those accompanying great earthquakes, can by no type of legitimate extrapolation be held to be incipient movements of the gigantic magnitude and intricate complexity that have been experienced by the earth at some time or times in the past. The erosion of deep gorges through solid rock by normal river flows, no less than the erosion of vast peneplains near sea level by ordinary stream action, are things which not only have no observational basis, but which seem to be precluded by the basic principles of stream mechanics.

All such events can only be explained by admitting that present-day phenomena are *not* adequate to account for them. The Flood theory also recognizes this, but postulates only one great physical revolution (chiefly diluvial in character, but also and necessarily

accompanied by great volcanic and telluric movements) far eclipsing anything ever experienced by the
earth before or since, followed by glaciation of tremendous extent, and perhaps also by the splitting and
spreading of continents.

The so-called uniformity theory ridicules the idea of
geologic cataclysm, while actually having to resort to a
great number of geological events and phenomena of a
character and intensity quite outside the scope of anything ever observed in the present age. Since this is the
case, it follows that the Flood theory is quite as consistent with a true scheme of uniformitarianism as is the
theory that has appropriated the name, and in many
ways much more so. The Flood theory furthermore has
very good basis in written and orally transmitted
records, whereas the presently accepted interpretation
of historical geology has no such basis at all.

There is surely no intention here to impugn either
the abilities or the motives of modern geologists. Most
of them are capable, sincere men, who are diligently,
sacrificially and honestly devoted to the study of earth
science. I myself have taken considerable graduate
work in geology and belong to all the important geological societies, and so can gladly testify to the above
statement.

Generally speaking, the adoption of the uniformity
theory by geologists has not necessarily been because
of an anti-religious bias, but because they believe it to
be the most scientific approach to geologic study. However, it seems very likely that the effect of their train-
ing in the uniformitarian tradition, together with the
long-time preponderance of geological opinion, has
been to keep them from ever even considering the possible merits of the diluvial theory.

Most of the results of the past hundred years of
geologic study and research would be valid regardless
of which theory is correct. None of the great mass of
useful geologic data or techniques would have to be

discarded if the Flood theory were accepted. Only the time element and the evolutionary implications would be sacrificed, and neither of these has any genuine value in geologic research.

As far as the evolutionary deductions are concerned, we have already examined somewhat the very dubious character of the entire philosophy of progressive evolution. The fact that the only real evidence supporting evolution comes from geology, and that all the other evidence of real biological change is much better evidence of deterioration would, by strong implication, make the evolutionary framework for geology exceedingly questionable. The other major item that would need to be revised in geology is the interpretation of the time involved in the formation of the strata. This also will be found to be a very questionable element in the theory, as usually held by orthodox geology. Methods of measuring geologic time and their dependability will be discussed later in the chapter.

There are other very positive evidences for the Flood which should be mentioned. The most outstanding of these are the enormous graveyards of fossils that are found all over the world. Almost without exception, the appearance and manner of preservation of the fossils indicate that they were buried suddenly; nothing of the sort is taking place now. It is known that such few fishes as die natural deaths are usually soon devoured in whole or partially by other creatures. In any event, they do not settle into the ocean or river bed but float on the surface until eaten or decomposed. A modern fish buried whole in sediment normally deposited would be a unique specimen. When land animals die, their remains are almost always quickly decomposed.

It is practically impossible today to find the bones of modern animals in the process of fossilization. How then can the ancient fossil deposits be accounted for on the basis of uniformity? The extent and wealth of these deposits is one of the marvels of geology. Fossil fish beds have been found which extend miles in every direction and contain fish buried in whole shoals by the millions. The fish have every appearance of having been buried alive and with great suddenness. The same is true of the reptilian deposits of the Rockies and the Black Hills and many other parts of the worlds. The amazing elephant beds of Siberia, the hippopotamus beds of Sicily, the horse beds of France and other parts of Europe, to say nothing of the shells of marine organisms, which probably form the greater part of the stratified deposits of the globe, all point to a great worldwide catastrophe in which ". . .the world that then was, being overflowed with water, perished" (II Peter 3:6). In no other way can the sudden extinction of the dinosaurs and the great mammals of the past be accounted for. They certainly could not have been eliminated by the smaller and much less hardy creatures of the present order in any struggle for existence.

The Siberian deposits of elephants, or mammoths, should be discussed further. Literally millions of these animals have been entombed in the vast wildernesses of that land. Some explorers have said that on some of the northern islands, particularly, the ground consisted almost entirely of mammoth bones. A regular trade in fossil ivory has afforded livelihood for the natives of this region since at least 900 A.D. In the more northern parts of the country, where the ground is perpetually frozen, a number of these beasts have been preserved whole, with even the skin and hair intact. From the congested blood in the blood vessels of these frozen elephants, scientists say they must have died by drowning, in spite of the fact that the modern elephant is a very strong and long swimmer. The remains of the last meal, consisting of elephant grass and other plants now utterly foreign to that region, have been found in their stomachs.

What is true of the mammoths is also true to a lesser

extent of many other animals whose fossil remains have been marvelously preserved in Alaska and Siberia. This is especially true of the rhinoceros, which is now as much a stranger to Siberia as is the elephant. These animals were very evidently then living in a land where the climate was warm and there was an abundance of vegetation. This was absolutely necessary to support the hordes of the animals that lived there. That they were suddenly buried by a great deluge, accompanied by a rapid and extreme change of climate, is very evident. No slowly encroaching glacial age or any of the tenets of modern evolutionary geology can account for these amazing finds.

The Siberian mummies are an especially vivid illustration of one outstanding fact that paleontology unquestionably reveals; that is, that at one time in the history of the globe there was a worldwide temperate climate. The remains of coral reefs formed by sea creatures that can live only in warm waters have been found so far north that it is now believed that they underlie the very poles themselves. Tropical animals have been found in large numbers as fossils not only in Siberia but in Greenland, Alaska, and practically every region in the world. Fossil ferns and other tropical and temperate vegetation have also been found in large numbers in the polar regions.

It is also generally accepted by geologists that the most recent geological epoch was actually an Ice Age, during which great ice sheets covered almost 30 percent of the world's land areas. However, uniformitarian geology has never been able to explain either the worldwide warm climate or the glacial epoch that followed it, though numerous theories have been proposed (and later rejected) for each. The Flood theory, on the other hand, provides the perfect explanation for both.

Another geologic evidence of the Flood is the existence of raised beaches and terraces, indicating former high water levels. These raised beaches and terraces are found all over the world, often hundreds and even thousands of feet above present water levels. They are found along coast lines, on the sides of river valleys, and along the shores of great inland basins, in truly worldwide distribution. There are a number of ways in which geologists have suggested these terraces might be formed. By far the most logical explanation for most of them is that they were formed by the waters of the Flood, possibly over many years, as the lands were uplifted and the waters receded. Rivers carried much greater discharges and the oceans were at a much higher level relative to the land than now. Lakes and inland basins formerly contained much more water and submerged far greater areas than at present. These facts surely can be understood far better in terms of post-deluge conditions than in any other way.

Finally, the very fact that most of the sedimentary rocks of the earth were obviously laid down under moving water, including the peaks of most of the great mountain ranges, is itself a strong indication of the Flood, although it has actually been made the basis of evolutionary geology.

The physical cause and character of the deluge must necessarily be somewhat a matter of speculation. There are, however, some very interesting possibilities suggested by the Genesis account of creation and the Flood.

It is intimated in the second chapter of Genesis (verse 5) that there was no rainfall, such as we know it now, in the antediluvian period. The rainbow was mentioned specifically (Genesis 9) as a divine token given to Noah by God after the Flood. This implies that atmospheric water, if any, was always in the vapor state before then and could not form a rainbow. The statement in the first chapter of Genesis (verse 7) that the "waters which were above the firmament" were separated during the creation from the "waters which were below the firmament" would indicate that at this time there was a great body of water vapor surrounding the earth above its atmosphere. The word "firmament" literally means "expanse" and would seem to be descriptive of at least the troposphere (the part of the atmosphere, located below the stratosphere, in which there are now convective currents, storms, clouds and raindrops).

Certain very unusual atmospheric and climatic conditions are also indicated by the extreme longevity of the antediluvians' lifespan. Such a condition is also strongly implied by the biblical record of a tremendous rain, continuing for 40 days and 40 nights, as one of the causes of the deluge. It is certain that present atmospheric and meteorologic conditions could never produce a universal rainstorm lasting for 40 days. There is only enough water vapor in the atmosphere at present to cover the lands to a depth of about an inch.

However, there is enough water in the oceans of the world to cover the entire earth to a depth of almost two miles if the terrestrial topography were smoothed to a common elevation. It is conceivable that some of the present oceanic water was, before the deluge, stored in a great vapor canopy surrounding the earth. It may have extended throughout the present stratosphere and ionosphere (the ionosphere is at present a vast layer above the stratosphere in which there are great numbers of atoms and molecules in an ionized state, and in which are produced many remarkable electrical phenomena), or may even have been largely outside the present bounds of these layers.

The condensation and precipitation of the canopy most likely was brought about by the breaking-up of the "fountains of the great deep," mentioned in Genesis 7:11 as associated with the "windows of heaven" in causing the Flood. This phrase strongly suggests the eruption of great quantities of volcanic materials and water from beneath the earth's primordial crust. The volcanic dust particles, combined with the upwelling turbulence, could well have provided the condensation nuclei and temperature changes necessary to induce the condensation and precipitation of the canopy.

Other possible causes for the precipitation of the canopy might be suggested, but it may be impossible to determine the complete explanation, in view of the greatly changed conditions of the present atmosphere.

This great canopy of vapor, if it existed, would have resulted in the physical phenomena that Scripture and geology indicate must have prevailed before the Flood. It would probably have been invisible to the inhabitants of the earth, but it would have intercepted and filtered out much of the short wave-length radiation, including ultra-violet and X-rays, and the mysterious and intensely powerful cosmic rays, that now reach the earth. In fact, the blanket of invisible water vapor that permeates the present atmosphere is the very thing that makes life possible on the earth. If the ultra-violet and cosmic radiation were not thus filtered before reaching the earth, they would quickly destroy all life.

The existence of the prediluvian "waters above the firmament" would have created a healthier physical environment than now exists on the surface of the earth. The canopy would have the effect of preventing extremes of heat and cold, resulting in a uniformly warm, probably sub-tropical, climate all over the globe. This phenomenon has already been demonstrated geologically by the discovery in polar regions of many evidences of former warm climactic conditions there.

The uniform climate, together with a probably much different and more gentle arrangement of topography, would have caused much different meteorological conditions. Winds and storms would have been impossible, since they result basically from temperature differences. It is unlikely that, though there would have been—by evaporation and transpiration—a continuous interchange of water near the earth's surface, rain as we know it now could have been produced. This inference is supported by the phenomenon mentioned in Genesis 2:5, 6: ". . . for the Lord God had not caused it to rain upon the earth, . . . But there went up a mist from the earth, and watered the whole face of the ground." With no water except the transparent water vapor in the air, the rainbow would have been unknown until after the Flood when its first appearance was as a beautiful and striking token of God's promise to Noah.

There may also have been great underground reservoirs of water under pressure, implied in the term "waters below the firmament," and in the later reference to the "fountains of the great deep." These would have had surface or underground outlets at certain places and thus maintained rivers. A sub-surface water table would support luxuriant vegetation everywhere.

It should be emphasized that these suggestions are merely suggestions; they are not specifically taught in Scripture. However, available meteorologic and geologic knowledge, together with the various biblical statements concerning antediluvian phenomena, all show striking harmony with the outlined theory, or some modification of it.

As we have seen in the preceding chapter, modern genetic research has demonstrated that new inheritable characteristics, not attributable merely to recombinations of factors already present in the genetic system, are caused chiefly by gene mutations. The same research has also demonstrated that these changes are nearly always deteriorations and that the occurrence of such mutations follows statistical laws. They seem to be caused by some disorganizing medium, especially short wave-length radiation, entering the chromosomes of the germ cells. The rate of mutation in a species, therefore, depends on the rate at which such rays will penetrate the germ cells, which in turn is statistically dependent on the amount of radiation entering the environment. Mutations, of course, occur in the body cells ("somatic mutations") as well as in the germ cells ("genetic mutations"), and an accumulation of somatic mutations in an individual has a definitely harmful effect on his health and longevity.

The antediluvian environment, as pictured above, would have had far less such radiation than does the present one. Therefore, there must have been fewer mutations. Everything favored the continued production of larger, stronger, longer-lived specimens in every type of creature. This, of course, is what we have already seen the fossil record to indicate. According to the Bible, many men lived to be over 900 years old. However, with the vapor canopy precipitated at the time of the deluge, the mutation rate speeded up, the size and strength of the average creature deteriorated, many species became extinct, and the length of the life span began a steady decline. These trends are still apparent today, although modern medical and sanitary science has, to a considerable extent, masked the natural trend as far as man is concerned.

This theory clarifies and makes more vivid the picturesque language of Genesis that ". . . the windows of heaven were opened." At the same time, ". . . the fountains of the great deep were broken up," implying a tremendous upheaval of the "waters that were under the firmament."

It is now easier to realize something of the overwhelming nature of this catastrophe. Certainly, every foot of the earth's surface must have been profoundly disturbed and altered. All creatures, except some of those at home in the water and all of those preserved by God in the Ark, must have violently perished, many being buried alive by the whirling sediments and debris. When, a year later, Noah and his family came out of the Ark, they saw a tremendously different world. No canopy of vapor filtered and diffused the sun's rays any longer and a rainbow appeared in the sky as a sign from God that this aqueous judgment would never again be visited on the earth (and, indeed, it could not if the upper waters were no longer there).

It is doubtless that this great event, if it occurred, would have been preserved not only in the rocks, but in the history and traditions of the race. That this is actually the case is known by every student of ethnology. Practically every country and tribe in the world has its own flood story, many of them amazingly similar to the biblical account—even in such details as the sending of the dove and the raven to search for land and the offering of sacrifices to the deity when the waters subsided. Yet the similarity is not so marked as to permit the idea that somehow the Genesis account had penetrated to all these scattered peoples. All of the stories, save that in Genesis, have been distorted with all sorts of impossible and absurd exaggerations. Since most of them were handed down by word of mouth, this is exactly what would be expected. Yet, they obviously all stem from the same historical event.

Flood stories have been found in every region in the world, except certain parts of Africa—including such widely scattered lands as China, Babylon, Wales, Russia, India, America (practically all Indian tribes), Hawaii, Scandinavia, Sumatra, Peru, Polynesia. Geologists who dogmatically affirm that the universal Flood is purely legendary have to ignore or explain away the powerful ethnological evidence.

The very peoples and population of the world are a convincing testimony to their origin from a common stock at about the time and place indicated in the biblical record. Archaeological evidence almost invariably indicates some point near the eastern shore of the Mediterranean as the cradle of civilization. The recorded or otherwise trustworthy history of nations elsewhere in the world always indicates either a migration from this area or else fades into oblivion at a time when Sumeria and other Middle Eastern nations are known to have been in an advanced stage of civilization.

Furthermore, assuming that the present human race originally sprang from two people, whether it was some ape-like dawn-man and his mate, or Noah and his wife, we find that the present population of the world supports the latter view and makes the former seem ridiculous.

The population of the world in 1800 has been estimated at about 850,000,000. It is now (1978) about four billion. We can say that the population has doubled twice in about the past 200 years. There is no objective reason to suppose that this rate of 100 years for the population of the world to double itself should have been significantly slower during other periods of history. In 1650, world population was only about 400,000,000. The present rate implies a considerably more rapid increase. Now, if the original population was two, we can find by logarithms that the population would have to have doubled itself approximately 31 times to produce the present number of people in the world. If the original pair lived, say, 500,000 years ago, which is considerably less than the average evolutionary estimate, the average interval for the doubling of the population would have been 16,000 years—which is absurd. If, on the other hand, all people are descended from Noah and his wife, who according to the Ussher chronology must have lived about 4,500 years ago, then the average interval for doubling is about 150 years—which is entirely reasonable.

One other phase of the Flood story has been subjected to a great deal of ridicule. It is charged that, even if Noah were able to build an ark in the primitive time in which he lived, it could not possibly hold representatives of every known species of living creature.

This charge is entirely unwarranted. In the first place, the dimensions of the Ark are not precisely known. The Bible gives the dimensions in terms of the measure of length called the cubit. There were several cubits used in ancient times and just what length in inches Noah's cubit had is a matter of speculation. It is believed that the most likely value is about 18 inches. If this is true, then it can be said that each of the Ark's three decks contained about 34,000 square feet of floor space. Since each deck was approximately 15 feet high, the smaller and medium-sized animals could have been placed in cages in tiers one on top of the other. The total carrying capacity of the Ark was then 1,500,000 cubic feet. Over 500 ordinary cattle cars could have been stored in the Ark. Certainly there was ample room in the Ark for all the animals that the Bible indicates were brought into the Ark, as well as plenty of food for them.

It is also true that Noah was not required to bring all the species of sea creatures into the ship, as the Flood would certainly not destroy all of them. The same could apply to such birds as live largely on the surface of the waters. Large species are comparatively few, of course, even among land animals. Furthermore, it is quite true that very many of what biologists call species are merely varieties and would not have been carried in the Ark. It is conceivable to the creationist that there has been considerable variation in the species, so much so as to possibly produce many varieties that have since become fixed and are classed as species in many classifications. It is even to be considered possible that, in some cases, the so-called families may have constituted the originally created kinds. This assumption can be justified partially, at least, on the basis of genetics and the fossil record; but certainly no links between the families, such as an animal intermediate between a dog and cat, can be predicated on the basis of modern knowledge. At any event, the old argument about Noah's Ark being too small is seen to have broken down completely. If any argument could be made against it, it would be that the Ark was larger than necessary.

The question of the age of the earth must be considered briefly before concluding this chapter. A literal reading of the Biblical record will yield a date of about 4,000 B.C. for the creation. On the other hand, geologists usually estimate the earth to be about five billion years old. This matter of geological dating is very important, both in estimating the earth's age and in fixing the absolute depositional date of the various formations. However, it is a very detailed and involved subject and one that cannot be adequately handled here in a brief treatment.

The chronometers most often used in the past have been the rate of cooling of the earth, the deposits of sediment at the mouths of rivers as compared with the sedimentary deposits on the earth's surface, rates of erosion of the earth's surface, the amount of salt and other chemicals in the ocean, and radioactivity. Scientists now readily admit that all of these, except possibly the last, are not at all to be trusted and are of practically no value in calculating the earth's age. This admission would most certainly never have been made had not the estimates based on these methods turned out finally to be far too low to permit the present state of the organic world to have been attained by evolution. It is true, however, that the estimate obtained by each of these methods was stretched beyond all justification, so that the errors caused by the weaknesses inherent in the methods themselves were of such nature as to give too large an estimate. Nevertheless, the methods were discarded when proved unsatisfactory to the theory of evolution.

For example, probably the best and most reliable of all the methods was the one based on the salt in the sea. The amount of sodium and other chemicals in the

sea is fairly well known, as well as the rate at which
the rivers of the world are emptying more such elements into the sea. It was then assumed that the rate
had always been the same and that originally there
was no sodium at all in the sea. Using these assump-
tions, which of course were wholly unwarranted and
unreasonable, the age of the earth was estimated as, at
the most, 100 million years (other elements give much
smaller ages). Since it is extremely probable that the
sea contained a great deal of sodium to begin with and
also that the rivers once were much larger than at
present and that the rate of erosion was much more
rapid, this estimate is seen to be enormously too large.
However, it has been discarded by evolutionary
geologists as being too small.

The only method that has been satisfactory to the
evolutionists is the radioactivity method. It is known
that metals of high atomic weight, such as thorium
and uranium, are constantly being broken down into
radium and eventually into an isotope of lead. The
rates of such decompositions are believed to be con-
stant. Consequently, when rocks are found containing
uranium, thorium, and lead, the relative amounts of
the metals in the rocks are taken as an index of their
age. However, there is no dependable way to estimate
how much uranium or thorium may have been leached
out of the sample. This is a common occurrence and, in
fact, many deposits of radioactive minerals have actually been rejected for age determinations because of
the belief that this had taken place.

Neither is there any way of knowing how much lead
may have been originally deposited with the uranium.
In fact, more often than not, samples are believed to
have been deposited in association with various
amounts of original "common" lead, though just why
this should be so is not at all evident. Certain very
delicate and precise measurements have to be made on
the sample by means of a mass spectrometer in order to

be able to estimate how much of this common lead has contaminated the sample. There are many questionable points about this procedure, but even assuming that the actual amount of common lead can be ascertained and deducted from the total in the sample, it is still quite unreasonable to affirm that the remaining radioactively derived lead may not have been also in part deposited initially with the parent metal uranium or thorium.

In fact, it is quite contrary to the whole tenor of historical geology to say that a deposit of radioactive metal could have remained unaffected by all the effects of telluric movements, igneous activity, ground water flow, chemical action, and other changes, for hundreds of millions of years or more, to be discovered near the surface in these present days. But if the deposit was affected by any agency during those unimaginably long periods of time, then it is manifestly untrustworthy as a means of measurement. The exact original amounts of metal must be known, and so must the exact amount of material produced by radioactive disintegration during all that time, in order for the age-estimate to have any meaning whatever. But it should be very evident that it is not only impossible to *know* that there have *never* been any disturbing factors, but it actually seems quite certain that there *must have been many*.

Furthermore, it should also be obvious that it can never be demonstrated for sure that the rate of disintegration has never changed during all those tremendous periods of time. Of course, if the rate has changed, then unless the exact way in which the change has operated is known, it is quite impossible to make any kind of valid age determination. It is known, of course, that the disintegration rate cannot be varied by great extremes of temperature or pressure, or by many other influences that have been brought to bear in the laboratory. Nevertheless, this does not prove that some other influence untried as yet might not change it. No one knows as yet just what causes the disintegration or why some materials have much greater disintegration rates than others—why, in fact, the rates of disintegration of some of the stages in the disintegration of uranium itself are infinitely more rapid than other stages in the same chain. Therefore, it is obvious that no one can know as yet just what influences might possibly affect the rate or may have affected it in the past.

As a matter of fact, it is known now that some disintegrations can be greatly hastened, and this is the basis of the atomic bomb. Furthermore, there now exists considerable evidence that the natural rate of disintegration may be affected by cosmic radiation, and possibly by still other influences not reproducible in laboratories.

In view of these and many more difficulties with the radioactivity method that might be enumerated, it is not surprising that results obtained by the method are so erratic. It is quite common to obtain widely divergent results from different samples in the same locality. Out of all the thousands of age determinations that have been made by this method, there are only a handful from all parts of the world that are considered to be fairly dependable and to fit satisfactorily into the accepted geologic time scale. Most of them have been rejected for one reason or another, quite often simply on the basis that the radioactivity age determination contradicts the geologic time-classification already worked out on the basis of the contained fossils.

All things considered, this method of estimating geologic time, no less than its predecessors, has been vastly overrated, and has been overburdened by the superstructure of geologic, astronomic, and philosophic interpretation that has been built upon it.

Thus, there is no really scientific proof yet offered that the earth is very old, and a truly objective geology would not suffer on this score by adopting the deluge hypothesis in place of the so-called uniformitarian framework.

There are a number of natural chronometers which are much more dependable and, as we might expect, give estimates that are very much shorter than the ones ordinarily quoted. Some of these are the decay of the earth's magnetic field, the amount of helium in the atmosphere, the amount of material from meteors that has fallen on the earth, and the amount of juvenile water produced by volcanoes and hot springs, all of which indicate that the earth is extremely youthful as compared with the estimates of the evolutionists.

This discussion might be considerably extended, but it can safely be said in summary that no genuine proof exists that the earth is very old. All methods of geological time measurement in current use are based on the theory of uniformity and ignore completely the possibility of an original creation and the effects of the Noachian Deluge. We are quite justified, scientifically as well as Scripturally, in maintaining the traditional position that the earth is not more than several thousand years old.

THE BIBLE
AND HISTORY

5

Probably no parts of the Bible have been more completely vindicated by modern discovery than those parts which deal with the history of the Jewish people and the nations with which they came in contact. It was once the custom of the critics to attack almost everything mentioned in the Bible as unhistorical, either written long after the events took place or else, as likely as not, simply fabricated by the writer. Since the multitude of archaeological discoveries made within the past hundred years, however, the pendulum is swinging the other way and the Bible is regarded even by those archaeologists who do not believe in its inspiration as an exceedingly trustworthy book from the historical standpoint.

It is well known that the earliest civilizations of the world were those of Sumeria, Egypt, Babylonia, Assyria, and other countries in the region near the eastern slopes of the Mediterranean. A tremendous amount of research has been applied to the study of the histories of these lands by modern archaeologists and historians. Their findings occupy literally hundreds of volumes, and we cannot begin to consider all of them here. However, I believe it would be helpful to look at a few of the more striking examples of the Bible's vindication by archaeology and related fields.

Some of the most interesting of the Babylonian and Egyptian discoveries, as well as those from more recent excavations in northern Syria, have to do with the period before the Flood. In these and other countries have been discovered numerous stories of the creation, the fall, the antediluvian patriarchs, and the Flood. Many of these stories bear striking similarities to the Bible accounts, and since many of them antedate the time of Moses, critics occasionally claim that Moses obtained his material from these sources. Consequently they say the Genesis record is merely legendary like the other stories. However, a comparison of the account in the Bible with the obviously mythological character of practically all these other stories is sufficient evidence that the record given in the Bible is incomparably superior to all other records combined. This fact can be accounted for only on the basis of inspiration.

It is only natural to suppose that some recollection of such important happenings as the creation and the Flood would be handed down by word of mouth to all the descendants of Adam and Noah, and it is extremely significant that in spite of their obviously legendary character, these spurious records show marked resemblance to the account given in the Bible. It seems certain that these stories must, therefore, have a definite factual basis.

The story of the dispersion of the peoples after building the Tower of Babel is usually ridiculed by Bible critics. Nevertheless, it is very likely that a part of the original tower is still standing. It has not been many years since what seemed to be the greatest of the Babylonian ziggurats was excavated. However, it was found from the Babylonian records that this tower was old during Babylon's heyday and had, in fact, been repaired and restored for use in her sacrificial worship. The Greek historian, Herodotus, about 500 B.C. described the structure, which then consisted of a series of eight ascending towers, each one recessed in turn, with a spiral roadway running around it as a means of climbing to the top. At the very summit was a great temple used in the worship of Babylon's gods. Babylonian legend that this tower was originally built by Nimrod coincides with the Bible record. In fact, the region is still called Birsnimroud by the Arabs. This great structure had a height of over 700 feet, of which several hundred still remain. If this tower is not actually the original Tower of Babel, it probably at least was meant to be a replica of it, as indeed may have been true of many of the other ancient Mesopotamian ziggurats.

It has been difficult to find direct archaeological evidence bearing on the early patriarchs of Israel before the time of Joshua. Of course, Israel was not yet a nation and it would be an extremely fortunate coincidence if relics of individuals such as Abraham, Isaac, Jacob, Joseph, or Moses would be found.

On the other hand, there is quite a bit of collateral evidence which illumines the biblical stories and proves that the descriptions of the countries, peoples, and general conditions of life during those times as given in the Bible are quite accurate. For example, Abraham's boyhood home is mentioned in the Bible as Ur of the Chaldees. The location and the very existence of this place were at one time uncertain, but in recent years it has been discovered and fully explored.

Critics at one time claimed that the Pentateuch could not have been written by Moses because the art of writing was unknown when he was living. Dis-

coveries in Ur and other places, however, have proven
that writing was well developed for at least many hundreds of years before even Abraham's time.

It is interesting to note that the "armchair theories"
of the higher critics about the gradual evolution of culture, science, religion, and civilization in general, are
gradually being demolished by each new archaeological
discovery. Recent explorations at great numbers of
these ancient cities have revealed over and over again
that the earliest discoverable civilizations were the
highest, and that there was often a degeneration in the
arts and sciences as time went on. It has even been
shown that their religion was originally monotheistic
and later degraded into polytheism, rather than the
other way around, as formerly claimed.

Recent discoveries (1964-1978) in northern Syria
have been particularly significant in illuminating the
book of Genesis. Over 17,000 tablets—in addition to
artifacts of many kinds—have already been excavated
at the site of ancient Ebla. The tablets contain hundreds of geographic names, historical references, allu-
sions to economic matters and descriptions of religious
and judicial practices, including an elaborate code of
laws. All of them date prior to the destruction of Ebla
by the Akkadians around 2250 B.C. (about 200 years
before Abraham).

The language of the tablets is a Semitic language
closely akin to both Hebrew and Phoenician. A number
of personal names found in the Ebla tablets are clearly
equivalent to various names in the book of Genesis
(though not the same individuals) including Esau,
David, Saul and Ishmael. The greatest king of Ebla
was a man named in the tablets as Ebrum, and this
might well be the same man as Eber (Genesis 10:21,
24, 25; 11:14-17), who is the man from whom the name
"Hebrews" was derived. Many Canaanite and Syrian
cities, familiar in the Old Testament, are mentioned in
the Ebla tablets. A creation tablet is more similar to

105

the Genesis creation record than any others yet discovered.

The invasion of a northern confederacy of kings into the land of Canaan at the time of Abraham and Lot (Genesis 14:5-17) has been fully confirmed by the archaeological investigation of Dr. Nelson Glueck, one of the outstanding Palestinian archaeologists of our generation. Although not a believer in the verbal inspiration of the Bible, Dr. Glueck had great confidence in its historical accuracy, maintaining that archaeology had never refuted a single one of its historical references, while it had confirmed large numbers of its statements.

Sodom and Gomorrah and the three "cities of the plain" near the southern end of the Dead Sea have also been excavated in recent years, along five rivers emptying from the east into the Dead Sea. These cities were evidently very prosperous. The tombs that have been uncovered indicated over a million people had been buried in them. Archaeological explorations at the site prove definitely that the region was inhabited during the time of Abraham, but immediately thereafter became barren of inhabitants and remained so for nearly two thousand years.

The Bible says Sodom and Gomorrah were destroyed by the raining of fire and brimstone (sulphur) from the sky. This sounds much like a volcanic eruption. The region formerly occupied by these cities on the shores of the Dead Sea has large quantities of sulphur and bitumen. This, along with the volcanic rocks and the sulphurous gases generated in the soil, all points back to some tremendous holocaust in the past.

Even the case of Lot's wife becomes clearer in the light of these facts. It is likely that she lagged behind (the probable meaning of "looked back") and was overcome in the catastrophe. There are huge beds of salt in the region, and it may be that she was buried by a mass of salt thrown in the air. The word translated "salt" does not necessarily mean sodium chloride, but might apply to any crystalline chemical compound. It is conceivable that she was buried by the lava and later, through the years and by the ordinary forces of nature, became petrified or fossilized, thus actually turning into "salt." This very thing is known to have happened to a great many individuals in the volcanic destruction of the city of Pompeii.

The Hebrew captivity in Egypt, as well as the Exodus, are now, because of archaeological evidence, accepted as historical even by critics. The ten plagues, although no directly corroborative evidence of them has yet been discovered, have attained added significance with the discovery that every one of them seemed particularly aimed at some phase of the religion of the Egyptians. The deities of the Nile, the goddesses of the frog, the fly, and the cattle, the gods of medicine, the elements, the sun, the fertility of the fields, and finally the goddess of birth, all suffered tremendous loss of prestige in the minds of the extremely polytheistic Egyptians because of the plagues of Jehovah. Archaeology, by thus revealing the religion of the Egypt of Moses' day, indirectly substantiates the Bible records and certainly endues them with greater meaning.

Some recent writers (Immanuel Velikovsky, Donovan Courville and others) have pointed out that a reduction of the standard Egyptian chronology by about 600 to 800 years, with an entirely different Pharaoh on the Egyptian throne at the time of the Exodus, will yield an actual Egyptian record of these plagues, as well as other corroborations of the biblical accounts from the Egyptian point of view. Since this proposed chronological revision has so far been either rejected or ignored by most Egyptologists, this particular confirmation of Old Testament history remains somewhat uncertain at this time.

Concerning the wanderings of the Israelites in the

wilderness, little of a secular nature is known other than that a people called Khabiri (possibly the Hebrews) began overrunning the countries of Canaan about this time. The conquest began with the crossing of the Jordan and the destruction of Jericho. Both events were accomplished by means of miraculous help from God. The Bible relates how, when the priests bearing the ark of the covenant stepped to the Jordan's edge, ". . . the waters which came down from above stood and rose up upon a heap . . . and the people passed over right against Jericho" (Joshua 3:16).

It is interesting that a similar thing has happened at least three other times in history, the last in 1927. Each time it has been caused by an upstream landslide, which left the river bed below dry for several hours. The Bible account could well describe a miraculously timed landslide and the resultant damming of the waters.

The story of the conquest of Jericho, which followed this crossing, may also have been vindicated by archaeology. At one occupation level, possibly corresponding to Joshua's time, the walls of Jericho were found to have literally "fallen down flat." It has been suggested that this was caused by an earthquake. Possibly so, but the event itself corresponds to the account in the Scriptures. Furthermore, it was found that the city itself had not been looted, as was the custom in those days, but burned, which further corresponds to the Bible account. There is some disagreement yet about the chronology, but some very competent archaeologists are satisfied this event is the same one described by Joshua.

Among the strongest of the peoples which the Hebrews had to face in the promised land were the Hittites. There are a great many references to these people in the Bible, but until the closing years of the 19th century, there was no external evidence that they ever existed. For many years, the higher critics used the Hittite legend as one of their most telling blows against the inspiration of the Scriptures. Archaeological scholarship, however, has now shown that these people constituted one of the most powerful and influential nations of antiquity. Once more the weakness of the critical position and the truth of the Bible has been demonstrated.

The same story might be told of Edom and the Edomites who are mentioned time and again in the Bible. They were completely forgotten in secular history until the 19th century when references to them were found in Egyptian and Assyrian monuments. Finally, the splendidly preserved remains of their capital city, Petra, "the rock city," were discovered. Thus, the critics, who had thought the Edomites to be legendary, were again defeated.

Jehovah's instruction that the Israelites exterminate the Canaanite inhabitants of the promised land has commonly been regarded as cruel and unjust. This event must now be viewed in the light of archaeological discoveries relating to the Canaanite civilization and religion. These discoveries have demonstrated that Canaan had degenerated into an area of unbridled wickedness and cruelty, including the use of child sacrifice and the grossest immoralities regularly practiced under the guise of religion.

In our modern world of permissiveness, the idea that God will punish sin is abhorrent to many people. The fact remains, however, that God is a holy God and will one day "be revealed from Heaven with His mighty angels, in flaming fire taking vengeance on them that know not God, and that obey not the gospel of our Lord Jesus Christ" (II Thessalonians 1:7, 8). The punishment of the Canaanites was merely a token of this coming judgment. In this case, it was actually an act of mercy, designed to spare generations yet unborn the terrible contamination and deadly influence of the Canaanite culture. Even the Canaanite children that were slain were better off (since children dying before the "age of accountability" are safe in Christ), while the adults had descended to such depths of idolatry and depravity as to be irreclaimable.

Many discoveries have also thrown light on the periods of the judges and the kings of Israel that strongly support the historical accuracy of the Old Testament accounts. What many believe were King Solomon's great stables have been unearthed, for example, as well as a great copper-smelting furnace belonging to Solomon at his seaport of Ezion-Geber. During the later period of the divided kingdom, the Assyrian Empire was in its ascendancy and power, and many discoveries in Assyrian archaeology also illumine and confirm the biblical histories. The failure of Sennacherib to take Jerusalem from King Hezekiah, in spite of the seeming invincibility of his mighty army, is implied in one of the Assyrian cylinders unearthed at the site of the ancient capital of Nineveh. Hezekiah's pool and conduit, constructed during this time probably in anticipation of the coming Assyrian siege, have been found still intact beneath Jerusalem.

These are only a few of the vast number of discoveries made in the past century that confirm the accuracy and authenticity of the Old Testament histories.

Problems still exist, of course, in the complete harmonization of archaeological material with the Bible, but none so serious as not to bear real promise of imminent solution through further investigation. It is extremely significant that, in view of the great mass of corroborative evidence regarding the biblical history of these periods, there exists today not one unquestioned find of archaeology that proves the Bible to be in error at any point. Truly this book is the Word of God!

It has long been one of the chief tenets of modernism that most of the canonical books of the Old Testament were written long after the events they purport to describe and usually by others than the traditional authors. As a consequence, they are said to contain many anachronisms and errors. There is no proof of an objective nature to support this claim, and yet the claim is almost always made in a very dogmatic way as one of the proven results of modern scholarship.

In particular, the Pentateuch and the book of Daniel have been maligned in this manner. By a critical examination of the words, phrases, and general style of the first five books of the Bible, critics have come to the conclusion that these books were written, not by Moses, but by several different writers, probably during the period just before or just after the Babylonian exile. This claim is made in spite of the fact that many of the New Testament writers and even Jesus himself refer to these writings as being of Mosaic authorship. These men lived much closer to the time of writing and were much better acquainted with their history than are modern critics. To deny the Mosaic authorship of the Pentateuch is to deny the deity of Christ. For if he was, as he claimed to be, the Son of God, surely he would not have spoken so frequently of Moses' writings as such if he knew Moses were not the author.

However, an unbiased examination of the books themselves surely must convince a reasonable person that they must have been written about the time of Moses. They abound with evidence of Egyptian influence. Even in the very early parts of Genesis, which are commonly supposed by the critics to have been derived from the Babylonian and Sumerian legends, there are many words, roots, and phrases that are very clearly borrowed from the Egyptian language. It is likely, however, that Moses drew on older records for the earlier sections of the book of Genesis, since there is no reason to doubt that the patriarchs could and would have written and transmitted the records of their own lives and their dealings with God. Moses was probably the editor, rather than the actual author, of these early records in Genesis. (See *The Genesis Record*, Grand Rapids, Baker Book House, 1976, pp. 25-30 for evidence supporting this view).

The story of Israel in Egypt, the Exodus, and the 40 years in the wilderness are very greatly steeped in Egyptian influence, of both a linguistic and a cultural nature. There are no demonstrably Persian or late Babylonian words. On the other hand, there are a number of archaic Hebrew forms which were not in use at all by the time the critics claim the Pentateuch was written. It is occasionally said that parts of these books contain Aramaic or late Hebrew words. However, it has been demonstrated that the great majority of such words are really root words common to all Semitic languages.

In fact, on the critical theory, it is impossible to understand why such a large portion of the writings would have been taken up with details of the Exodus and the wilderness wanderings. For example, why did the supposed post-exilic writers take so much time and space to describe the most minute details of the construction of the tabernacle in the wilderness and the forms of worship to be used in connection with it? Most of the critics used to claim that the tabernacle never even existed.

It is impossible to imagine why these writers would have gone to such great pains to deceive people by clothing their writings with a spurious antiquity and claiming them to be the works of Moses. How was it possible that no one, down through all the centuries, seems to have had the slightest suspicion that these writings were not genuine works of Moses until the modern higher critics went to work on them? It would be truly amazing if the channel through which has come the highest code of morals in the world and the purest revelation of God should have been contaminated by fraud at its source. If they were not really what they were represented to be it seems quite impos-

sible that the books could have been received as
genuine any time after that of Moses. They contain
detailed instructions as to laws and civil and ecclesias-
tical ordinances, which are presented as having been
in force from the time of Moses. They reveal the events
that initiated the institution and continued observance
of the Passover, which, according to the records, had
been observed from the time of Moses. Neither the
book, laws, priesthood, nor ordinances could ever have
been accepted at a later date if they were not actually
existing at that time, and believed by the people to
have been continually in force from the time of Moses.

Naturally, in a work of this nature, we cannot dwell
upon the details of the evidence for and against this
critical theory of the authorship of the Pentateuch and,
for that matter, other sections of the Old Testament as
well. However, for the student who is interested in the
subject, a wealth of literature is available. Every claim
and dogmatism of the critics has been adequately answered and refuted by Christian scholars.

Let us briefly consider the book of Daniel, however.
Probably not even the books of Moses have been subjected to as much criticism and as many charges of
spurious antiquity as has this book. However, this was
to be expected because of the amazing prophecies in
the book. Since many of them have been fulfilled with
meticulous accuracy, it is claimed that the book of
Daniel was written after the events had already occurred. If the genuineness of Daniel were admitted, the
fulfillment of its prophecies would constitute incon-
trovertible proof of its supernatural inspiration and by
inference establish the fact that all of the Bible had
been given by inspiration of God. Some of these
prophecies and their fulfillments will be discussed in
the next chapter.

The book purports to have been written over a rather
long period of time, but all during the Jewish exile in
Babylon. It is written partially in Aramaic and par-

tially in Hebrew. Those portions that especially concerned the captive Jews were written in Hebrew and those addressed especially to the Babylonians and their king Nebuchadnezzar, in Aramaic.

However, the book contains three Greek words and this fact was once used as the basis of the assertion that the book could not have been written until after the conquest of Babylon by Alexander the Great. Archaeology, however, has proven beyond any doubt that there was extensive commerce between Greece and Babylon even before the time of Nebuchadnezzar. It is known that at least one of the words in question (all three of which were the names of Greek musical instruments) was the name of an instrument which had been in more or less common use in Babylon for many years before the time of Daniel.

The existence in Daniel of eight Sumerian words would seem definitely to establish the time of writing as not later than Nebuchadnezzar's reign, for this language was never used after that and was almost a dead language even at that time. Even the Hebrew language was no longer used commonly after the captivity; so the fact that much of the book is written in Hebrew would imply that it was written before or during the captivity.

Considerable archaeological evidence has been brought to light that indirectly reveals the genuineness of the setting of the book of Daniel in the Babylon of Nebuchadnezzar and Cyrus. Excavations on the site of ancient Babylon have unearthed a building, the inscriptions on which show that it was used for the instruction of captive princes and nobles in the learning of the Chaldeans. This proves that the gracious treatment received by Daniel and his three friends was not foreign to Babylonian policy, as critics had claimed.

A huge furnace was discovered with inscriptions to the effect that it was used to burn those who refused to worship the gods of the Babylonians. This shows that the story of the three Hebrews in the fiery furnace at least had its basis in fact. A large pit was discovered which was used for feeding men who disobeyed the decrees of the king to the wild beasts. There was even a list of the ones who had been slain there, but Daniel's name was not among them. An inscription, made by Nebuchadnezzar himself, was discovered which contained a strange story which many archaeologists are convinced corresponds to the period of the king's madness described by Daniel.

The most serious criticism of Daniel has lain in its alleged historical inaccuracies. According to Daniel, Belshazzar was king of Babylon at the time of the conquest of the Persians. He was slain on the night of his drunken feast when the Persian army, under Darius the Mede, captured Babylon. But secular history said that Nabonidus was king of Babylon at the time. Furthermore, he was not slain but carried away captive by the Persians. Of course, the critics made the most of this very obvious error, maintaining that Belshazzar was merely a non-existent person invented by some later writer who was unfamiliar with history.

But through the years a great abundance of archaeological evidence has been accumulated which establishes beyond all doubt that Belshazzar actually did exist. He was the son of Nabonidus and, as a sort of regent over Babylon, served in the place of his father who was away from the city at the time of the Persian conquest. In other words, both Nabonidus and Belshazzar were kings of Babylon at that time. Archaeology has also revealed that Belshazzar actually was killed in his palace by the Persians on that fateful night.

The existence of Darius the Mede was also unknown to secular history for a long time, but archaeology has shown that the references to him are also most plausible. Although his name as given in the Bible has not yet been unearthed by archaeologists at least two men have been studied whose duties and acts would fit very well with Daniel's description of Darius. Daniel's account is now regarded by even the most critical as excellent history. A monograph by Dr. John Whitcomb, *Darius the Mede* (Grand Rapids, Eerdmans, 1959, 79 pp.), has shown beyond reasonable question the historical accuracy of this section of the book of Daniel.

Nevertheless, critics still aver that Daniel was written much later than the time of the captivity. This position, as mentioned before, is forced upon them by their dogmatic denial of the possibility of predictive prophecy. In the 11th chapter of the book there is a very remarkable and detailed prophecy of the histories of Persia, Greece, Egypt, Syria, and the Jews down to the time of Antiochus Epiphanes. Therefore, it is usually said that the book must have been written soon after the time of Antiochus, about 170 B.C. This is about the latest date that the critics dare to assign to the book for several reasons that we cannot consider here. As a matter of fact, though, they are inclined to overlook entirely the fact that Daniel contains many remarkable prophecies which were not fulfilled until much later than this date, including a description of the rise and fall of the Roman Empire and a prediction of the very nature and even the date of the coming Messiah. We shall discuss these in more detail later. It is clear that even if Daniel was written in 170 B.C. it is still a book of marvelous prophecy and the critics have defeated their own ends.

The book of Isaiah also contains many marvelous prophecies, which were later fulfilled. Therefore, it has been divided by the critics into at least two divisions, assigned to different authors at different periods of history, in spite of an abundance of external testimony and evidence against this notion. Jesus quoted from both of the two main divisions of Isaiah, and attributed both to the one prophet Isaiah (e.g. Matthew 4:16; 12:17).

The discovery in 1948 among the "Dead Sea Scrolls" of a very early copy of the book of Isaiah was given wide publicity in the popular press. This manuscript has been dated at no later than 100 B.C., earlier by many centuries than any other extant Old Testament manuscripts. In view of this, it is very significant that the manuscript is in all important particulars identical with the received Isaiah text and bears a striking testimony to the care and accuracy with which the Hebrew scribes copied and transmitted the Scriptures. Most of the few differences that do exist are merely matters of spelling, and there are no discrepancies of any real significance at all. There is no indication whatever that the scribe regarded the book as being divisible into two main parts, or composed by different authors.

It is interesting also that three sections of the book of Daniel were found together with the Isaiah manuscript. They have also been dated at about 100 B.C., and similarly substantiate the received text of these portions of Daniel. The few differences that exist are again mostly mere matters of spelling. Eventually, practically the entire Old Testament was found among these Dead Sea Scrolls, all of it practically identical to the received text.

We could fill several chapters with details of how the Old Testament has been and is being vindicated in a most wonderful way by the finds of archaeology. But let us consider briefly some of the discoveries of modern research in archaeology and textual criticism which bear on the historicity and trustworthiness of the New Testament.

Although it was formerly suggested by some critics that Jesus was entirely a legendary character, in recent years such a mass of evidence to the contrary has been compiled that no informed person doubts any longer that Jesus actually lived. Numerous inscriptions and papyri have been discovered that either mention the name of Christ as the leader and founder of the sect of the Christians or that simply refer to the Christians and their amazingly rapid growth. Many of these date from the first or very early second centuries, and it is impossible to suppose that they all resulted from the devotion of a group of fanatics to a legendary character.

It has also been well established now that the books of the New Testament are completely authentic from the standpoint of authorship and antiquity. It was formerly thought that many of the books, if not all, were written long after the time of Jesus by other than the traditional authors. This indictment was aimed not so much at the Pauline writings as at the Gospels, especially John, and at the Acts. In Acts it was long supposed that there were numerous gross historical inaccuracies and that, in fact, the whole tenor of the book belonged to a much later time than the days of the Apostles. However, archaeology has very completely refuted this claim. Practically all the towns and cities mentioned in Acts or in the Gospels have been located, with the finds at all these places being of such nature as to wholly vindicate the historical accuracy of the Scriptures. There are many remains of the architecture of Herod throughout Palestine, although his temple in Jerusalem was completely destroyed by the Romans in 70 A.D. Well-preserved relics of a synagogue have been explored on the site of Capernaum. It is possible that this was the very synagogue in which Jesus occasionally preached. Of course, there are a great many other sites and structures that are connected by tradition with Jesus and the Apostles, but in most cases these can be neither proven nor disproven.

Miniature images of Diana, such as described by Luke in the Acts, have been unearthed in Grecian cities. The remains of the Areopagus, or Mars' Hill, from which Paul delivered a sermon, may still be seen and an altar dedicated to "the unknown God" has also been discovered.

Inscriptions have been found in great abundance, some of which seem to contain the names of people actually mentioned in the New Testament. Many Roman coins have been found, including the Roman penny bearing Caesar's likeness. This is what Jesus was referring to when He said, "Render to Caesar the things that are Caesar's, and to God the things that are God's" (Mark 12:17). Inscriptions have been found describing the Roman census, which was taken, it seems, about every 13 years. During one of these, Luke states, Jesus was born. Criticism long maintained that this was a serious historical error because there was no record of any Roman census at a date that early. Later discoveries have revealed otherwise, however, and it is now known that the census had been an established custom for many years previous.

All of these finds, as well as many others, date from Apostolic times, and give the historical portions of the New Testament a definite vindication. Even when attacked from a linguistic angle, the New Testament has emerged victorious. The oldest New Testament manuscripts extant were written in a form of Greek unknown to classical literature. A great many words were late-dated by the critics. However, it is known now, from the many papyri inscriptions dating from the first century and earlier, that this peculiar language, now known as Koine Greek, was the universal language of the common people of the Mediterranean world during the time of Christ and the Apostles.

The book of John has been subjected to great criticism through the centuries, probably because of its superb presentation of Jesus as the Messiah, Son of God. Modern critics have dated its composition at some three or four centuries after Christ, because, they said, its peculiar theology belonged to that period rather than to the first century. However, many early second-century writers refer to or quote from John's Gospel. Evidence shows that it was composed by John himself no later than 95 A.D.

A papyrus fragment of a part of John's Gospel was found in 1935. All authorities date this at least before 150 A.D. This has demonstrated conclusively that this Gospel could not have been written later than about 100 A.D. Similar papyrus evidence demonstrating the first century origin of the other Gospels has also come to light.

There remains, however, the question of whether the events described in the books, especially those involving miracles, ever really took place. Were they fabricated by the writers to aid the spread of a new religion? Along with this question may be placed the question as to whether the character and life of Jesus were really as perfect as represented.

It will, I think, be conceded that all the facts of the New Testament record—the virgin birth, the miracles, the transfiguration, the sinless life—stand or fall with the truth or falsity of Jesus' resurrection from the dead. If Jesus died and rose again, which is the central and foundational belief of all true Christianity, then he must in truth have been God, and there remains no rational difficulty in believing the other things. In the light of his resurrection these things become, in fact, quite necessary.

Well, *did* Jesus of Nazareth rise from the dead? To deny it means to deny on a priori grounds the specific testimony of six of the eight New Testament writers. The other two definitely imply their belief in and knowledge of the resurrection. As we have seen, these witnesses are all established as to date and authenticity.

The descriptions of the resurrection morning and the later appearances of Christ in the four Gospels and in Acts do not have the character of manufactured evidence. The differences in the accounts (which, however, are not contradictory but complementary) alone prove this. The different accounts would almost necessarily have been the same if the writers had connived on the tale. The apostle Paul, acknowledged even by his critics to have been a man of great intellect and discernment, states that he was instantaneously changed from a Pharisee of the Pharisees to a Christian at the sight of the resurrected Christ. His great life and works prove the genuineness of his conversion. He states, in his first letter to the Corinthians, that more than 500 people saw the risen Lord on one occasion, many of whom were still living when he wrote.

There can be little doubt that Jesus actually was crucified and was dead when he was placed in the tomb. The Roman soldier thrust a sword into his side to assure himself that he really was dead, and out flowed blood mixed with water—possibly evidence of a hemorrhage in the heart cavity. He was placed in a tomb, covered from head to foot with grave clothes and a Roman guard was set to watch the sealed tomb. It is unthinkable that he could merely have been in a sort of coma and could have recovered sufficiently in the tomb to remove the grave clothes and walk out. Yet, it is also a fact of history that the tomb was empty early on the first day of the week following his crucifixion. The Pharisees and the Sadducees would certainly have produced the body if they could have done so in order to halt the rapidly growing Christian faith. And this rapid growth (there were over 3,000 converts in one day at Jerusalem on the day of Pentecost) can only be explained by the fact that these people believed that the tomb of Christ was empty and also, for that matter, that many had seen him since his resurrection.

But it might be argued that the soldiers had fallen asleep and the disciples actually stole the body of Jesus from the tomb. This is the story the Pharisees bribed the Roman soldiers to tell. Of course, even if the soldiers of the watch *were* sleeping on duty, that very fact would have made it impossible for them to see the disciples steal the body; so no real proof could be offered.

It is unthinkable that the greatest spiritual force and power for righteousness that the world has ever seen could have been founded on an intentional deception. The very change in the character of the disciples themselves gives the lie to this blasphemous charge. Men who had been weak, vacillating, and doubting suddenly became bold, powerful Spirit-filled proclaimers of the Gospel of Salvation through faith in the risen Christ. They had nothing of a material sort to gain from any such deception. They were persecuted and regarded as mad fanatics, and most of them were finally put to death in the great Herodian and Roman persecutions. The uniform testimony of even the enemies of Christianity down through the centuries has been that the Apostles and the thousands of other Christians that have been slain for their faith in Christ all died gloriously and unafraid. Men do not die like this for something they know to be a lie.

The very existence in the world of the Christian institutions of the Church, the observance of Sunday and the observance of Easter, all testify to the literal truth of the physical resurrection of Christ from the dead. All of these institutions can be traced back to about 30-40 A.D. Something extraordinary must have happened at that time to give them a start. The Sabbath, for example, was one of the most rigidly observed of the Jewish laws and customs. Most of the early Christians had been very devout Jews. How is it possible, apart from the resurrection, to explain the sudden change from Saturday to Sunday for the religious services of these people?

The impact of Jesus Christ upon the world's history in the past nineteen hundred years is itself a unique testimony to his Deity. There are some people who have thought this influence was harmful, citing certain evil practices or doctrines promulgated or con-

doned by certain segments of organized Christianity,
especially during the Middle Ages and Renaissance
period.

But true Christians, according to Scripture, are
those who have received the Lord Jesus by faith as
their Savior from sin. In most cases the harmful things
done in the name of Christ are chargeable to men or
groups who are not truly Christian in the biblical
sense. The great majority of men who have honestly
thought on the matter have recognized that the impact
of Christ and his followers upon the world has been
ennobling and uplifting to a degree far surpassing that
of all other teachers and philosophers.

The souls and lives of numerous men and women
have been redeemed from sin, fear, despair and misery
to lives of peace, holiness, and love. The morality of
whole continents has been purified and elevated by the
Christian gospel. Schools, hospitals, and benevolent
institutions of all kinds for the alleviation of suffering
and advance of true knowledge have been by-products
of Christianity wherever the Gospel has gone. Jesus
Christ has been the inspiration and theme for the
world's greatest music, art, and literature.

That all this, and much more, should result from the
life and teaching of an obscure Jewish carpenter would
be more miraculous and inconceivable than that he
should be, as he claimed, God's only and eternal Son.

Humanly, he was born in a stable in a small village,
and was brought up in another village. His hometown
was despised even by his Jewish countrymen and the
Jews themselves were then, as they have always been,
despised by most other peoples of the world. He had
little formal education, no obvious cultural talents, no
financial position and no political stature. He never
wrote a book or led an army or held any position in
government or industry or education. He taught a
small, motley, unpromising group of followers his doctrines, and made seemingly strange and impossible as-

sertions and promises. Then, after only three and a half years of such teaching, he was unjustly crucified and died as a common criminal on a Roman cross.

Yet it was this Man who made statements which, if he were only a man, must immediately have stamped him a preposterous liar or a mad fanatic. For example, he said on one occasion: "I am the light of the world: he that followeth me shall not walk in darkness, but shall have the light of life" (John 8:12).

If any mere man should ever say such a thing, it would immediately be interpreted by most sensible people as colossal conceit or even rank madness, especially if his human circumstances were those of Jesus'. Yet the amazing thing is that for 2,000 years this statement coming from him has sounded natural and true and trustworthy and, in fact, has been demonstrated to be a marvelously fulfilled prophecy. For 2,000 years he *has* been the light of the world, inspiring all those institutions, individuals and motives which have most contributed to all that is worthwhile in our present world. Those who have followed him have *not* walked in darkness, but *have* had the light of life, and there are millions upon millions who have testified so. Many have willingly and gladly followed him into places of hardness, even death, with no motive except love for him who died that they might have everlasting life.

It was also he who said: "Upon this rock [that is, upon that belief in himself as the Son of God], I will build my church; and the gates of hell shall not prevail against it" (Matthew 16:18). This is also quite a ridiculous statement if made by one who was only a man, but the centuries have revealed its prophetic realism. Against the Church of Jesus Christ (that is, the remarkable institution of a local body of believers who have taken Christ into their minds and hearts as Savior and Lord) have been hurled all the weapons of destruction that hell could conceive—the force of empires, relentless and bloody persecution, intellectual rationalism (which is even more deadly)—and, worst of all, the great burden of sin and indifference in the Church itself. And yet they have not prevailed against it, even as he promised!

And again, he said: "Heaven and earth shall pass away, but my words shall not pass away" (Matthew 24:35). What a preposterous, presumptuous, outrageous claim for any man to make! But now, in the 20th century, more than a few are fearing the earth's imminent destruction through atomic warfare. Biblical signs of the coming end of the age are numerous. Yet Jesus' words are more widely distributed and believed by more people than ever before. More books have been written about him and his words, by far, than those of any other man.

Through the centuries men have acclaimed him as the world's greatest teacher and its most perfect man. In the light of all this, what reasonable conclusion is possible but that he is all that he claimed, and can and will fulfill all his marvelous promises to those who believe on him?

The very center of his mission, his teaching, and his Gospel was the redemption of man from sin, through his own sacrificial, atoning death for man's sin. The completion of all this is guaranteed by his bodily resurrection from the dead, which has been declared again and again, by men trained and competent in the analysis of evidence, to be the best-demonstrated fact of all ancient history.

Thus, the Christian worships not a dead prophet or teacher or leader, but the living Son of God, whose bodily presence at the right hand of the Father in Heaven is affirmed in Scripture, and whose spiritual presence in the Christian's own heart offers further and final daily attestation to the great fact of Christ's resurrection.

FULFILLED PROPHECY AND INTERNAL EVIDENCES

6

The greatest demonstrable evidence for the inspiration of the Scriptures, apart from the conviction of personal experience, lies in the fact that hundreds of prophecies contained in its pages have been remarkably fulfilled. In attempting to refute the evidence from predictive prophecy, critics have either ignored the fulfillments, or sought to explain them away as coincidences, or have arbitrarily late-dated the writing so the prophecies appear to have been made subsequent to their fulfillment. These attempts, however, have always been based on a process of rationalization rather than on demonstrable fact.

Biblical prophecy, especially in the Old Testament, almost invariably centers around the nation of Israel and those peoples that come into close contact with the Jews. Most of the ancient nations in this category were exceedingly wicked and idolatrous and either were enemies of Israel or had a decidedly bad influence on her morals and spirituality. Consequently, the Holy

Spirit led the ancient prophets to make a number of predictions of coming judgment on these nations, predictions that have since been most remarkably fulfilled.

For example, consider the prophecy against that great city of antiquity, Tyre of the Phoenicians. It is found in the 26th chapter of Ezekiel and first describes the coming capture of the city by Nebuchadnezzar (verses 7-11). This was later fulfilled quite literally. However, the judgment forecast in verses 4 and 5 (". . . they shall destroy the walls of Tyrus and break down her towers: I will also scrape her dust from her, and make her like the top of a rock. It shall be a place for the spreading of nets in the midst of the sea. . .") seemed unfulfilled. History tells us that most of the people of Tyre escaped with their valuables to an island half a mile from the shore, where they built a new Tyre which was still great and powerful for almost 250 years.

But finally Alexander the Great finished what Nebuchadnezzar had begun. During his campaign of conquest through the East, the people of Tyre refused to surrender to him. There was no way for Alexander's armies to reach the island city to capture it so they built a causeway from the mainland. The Macedonians then literally "scraped the dust" of the old mainland city and ". . . laid [her] stones and. . .timber and. . .dust in the midst of the water" (Ezekiel 26:12) to build the causeway. (Note the change from the "he," Nebuchadnezzar, in verse 11 to "they" in verse 12, indicating different conquerors.) The causeway was thus built from the remains of the old city and the island city was captured and sacked.

Ezekiel 26:21 says: "I will make thee a terror, and thou shalt be no more: though thou be sought for, yet shalt thou never be found again, saith the Lord God." The mainland city of Tyre, against which the prophecy was directed, was never rebuilt. The site can be located only by following the directions of ancient historians for there aren't even any ruins or mounds to mark the spot. The causeway and island now form a desolate peninsula, used only by fishermen for the purpose of "spreading their nets" out for drying.

Tyre's sister city of Sidon had the following prophecy uttered against her: "Behold, I am against thee, O Zidon . . . For I will send into her pestilence, and blood into her streets; and the wounded shall be judged in the midst of her by the sword upon her on every side" (Ezekiel 28:22, 23). No fate of extinction was foretold for Sidon and even today it is a city of about 20,000. However, it has had one of the bloodiest histories any city ever had. It was almost destroyed by the Persians, was the scene of many fierce battles during the Crusades, and during the wars between the Druses and the Turks, and later between the Turks and the French. In 1840, Sidon was again the scene of bloodshed when it was bombarded by the fleets of three nations.

Two sister cities, close together and equal in importance, were thus the subjects of two very different prophecies. Each has been fulfilled to the letter. That would have been impossible except as directed by God, who alone "declares the end from the beginning" (Isaiah 46:10).

Yet that is just an isolated example. Consider also the city of Babylon. The great Babylonian nation and especially its capital city were the subject of many prophecies of divine judgment. Anyone reading a description of ancient Babylon must stand amazed at its immensity and strength. It seems that such a city should have lasted forever. Yet some of the prophecies against this city were—

And Babylon, the glory of kingdoms, the beauty of the Chaldeans' pride, shall be as when God overthrew Sodom and Gomorrah. It shall never be in-

habited, neither shall the Arabian pitch tent
there; neither shall the shepherds make their
flocks to lie down there. But wild beasts of the
desert shall lie there; and their houses shall be
full of doleful creatures; and ostriches shall dwell
there, and wild goats shall dance there. And
wolves shall cry in their castles and jackals in the
pleasant palaces (Isaiah 13:19-22, A.S.V.).

A great many other prophecies were directed against
the great city, giving additional details of the doom
that was to befall her. Yet all of them remained unfulfilled for centuries after they were written. Some two
centuries after Isaiah wrote his prophecy, Babylon was
captured by the Persians. Later it was ruled by the
Greeks, the Parthians, and the Romans, yet it continued to be a great city for centuries. It was still occupied during the time of Christ, although most of its
greatness had disappeared by then. But finally, re-
lentlessly, utter desolation crept over it until now,
every one of the prophecies has been accurately fulfilled. It is nothing but a great mass of shapeless heaps
and ruins, entirely uninhabited save by wild animals,
snakes, and insects. In the past, it has been the source
of great treasure to explorers who have rifled the
ruins, and its bricks and stones are still used for building in cities nearby. But Babylon itself is utterly desolate.

Many other cities have been singled out by the
prophets. We could not begin to discuss here the detailed fulfillment of all these predictions. However,
some of the cities and the corresponding prophecies are
listed below for the reader's reference:

Thebes, Egypt (the "No" of Scripture)—Ezekiel
30:14-15.

Memphis, Egypt (the "Noph" of Scripture)—Ezekiel
30:13.

Ashkelon, Philistia—Zechariah 9:5.

Ekron, Philistia. Also Gaza, Philistia—Zephaniah 2:4.

Bethel—Amos 3:14, 15.

Samaria—Micah 1:6, 7.

Jericho—Joshua 6:26.

Capernaum, Bethsaida, and Chorazin—Matthew 11:20-23.

All these and many other prophecies directed against specific cities either have been or are being fulfilled with meticulous accuracy.

Many countries, also, have been the subject of prophecy. Edom, or Idumea, was located next to Palestine. Although the Edomites were descended from Esau and were thus related to the Israelites, they were extremely idolatrous and treacherous and were almost constantly at war with the Hebrew nation.

Their land was very rugged and their capital city, Petra, had a seemingly impregnable position in the rocks of the mountains. It was a very great and rich city, being the terminus of one of the great trade routes of the East. Even today its ruined buildings and palaces, carved out of the solid rock, are most imposing and magnificent. But in Ezekiel 35:3-9, Jeremiah 49:16-18, and other places, there were predictions of the ultimate overthrow of Edom. Edom was to be an utter desolation; her trade was to cease, and all her inhabitants were to disappear. For many centuries after they were written, these prophecies remained in the Scriptures without being fulfilled. Even for some 600 years after Christ, Edom and Petra remained great and prosperous. But somehow, sometime, a change came. No one seems to know the story. Now the whole land of Edom, as far as the city of Maan, is utterly desolate. There are practically no human inhabitants and very little animal life. It is interesting that only Maan, a town on the east of Edom and the Temaan of Scripture, has escaped the desolation. But this is precisely what was predicted in Ezekiel 25:13: "I will make it a desolation from Temaan."

A similar judgment of permanent extinction was predicted for the Philistines, another great and war-like people of antiquity. They lived on the coast west of the Israelites and were almost constantly fighting with them. It was from the Philistines that much of the Jewish trouble with idolatry was derived. Consequently, we have the prophecy in Zephaniah 2:5, 6 (A.S.V.): ". . .the word of Jehovah is against you, O Canaan, the land of the Philistines. I will destroy thee, that there shall be no inhabitant. And the seacoast shall be pastures, with cottages for shepherds and folds for flocks."

There are several other similar prophecies against the Philistines, including some directed against specific Philistine cities, as noted before. As late as the 12th century A.D. the country still was strong and had many strong cities. The country has not been incorporated into the modern state of Israel but, until that time, the ancient land of the Philistines had been used for many centuries almost exclusively for grazing and agriculture.

The nation of Egypt, on the other hand, was not doomed to extinction, as were Babylonia, Edom, Philistia, and others. Egypt was one of the greatest powers of the ancient world. In passage after passage of Scripture, she was threatened with a gradual and permanent decline, though not with extinction. Ezekiel 29:15 says: "It shall be the basest of the kingdoms; neither shall it exalt itself any more above the nations: for I will diminish them, that they shall no more rule over the nations." Today that prophecy still stands unchallenged. The kingdom existed until recently and some of the people of Egypt today are the direct descendants of those who were at one time the greatest people in the world. Yet it was truly the basest of kingdoms. Though Egypt still seeks leadership among the Arabic peoples, it has no more exalted itself above the nations. There are a great many other predictions regarding Egypt, concerning such miscellaneous details as its industries, the weavers, the fisheries, the papyrus plants, the rivers and canals, its rulers, its exploitation by outsiders and the general desolation of the country. These have every one been fulfilled.

We shall not attempt to discuss most of these predictions here, but should mention that such countries as Moab, Ammon, Chaldea, Assyria, Ethiopia, and others are the subject of Biblical prophecies, all of which have been fulfilled.

We should consider briefly the Jewish people, however. The entire history of Israel has been foretold in the Bible in a very great number of prophecies, most of which have already been fulfilled. In the 28th chapter of Deuteronomy, even before the Israelites had entered the promised land, Moses predicted their future happiness in the land, their sufferings and punishment for disobedience, and finally their great worldwide dispersion. In the 30th chapter, he promised their eventual return, a prophecy which seemed impossible only a few decades ago, but which is now being marvelously fulfilled.

Their dispersion was prophesied by many others, including Christ himself, as well as the terrible persecution that would be theirs in all nations. But it was also revealed that they would not be destroyed or assimilated and that their national identity would be retained. Their eventual restoration as a nation, while still in unbelief, is indicated in Ezekiel 37 and other Scriptures. Though it was after "many days" (as prophesied in Hosea 3:4), eventually Israel was indeed established as a recognized nation (in 1948) and even regained its ancient capital of Jerusalem in 1967.

The book of Daniel contains what are usually regarded as the most marvelous prophecies in the Bible. In chapters 2, 7, 8 and 11 of this book, the entire his-

tory of the world is foretold, from the time of
Nebuchadnezzar to the end. The careers of Babylonia,
Medo-Persia, Greece, Egypt, Syria, and Rome are described with such wealth of description and detail that
no one acquainted with the facts of history can be uncertain as to the events and nations referred to. This
very minuteness of detail is, in fact, the crutch that
critics lean on to contend that the book of Daniel had to
have been written after these events had transpired.
The rationalism of the critics rules out the miracle of
predictive prophecy, so this contention is necessary for
them. Although they still cling to this idea it has been
almost irrefutably proven, as we saw earlier, that the
book is authentic both as to date and author. Thus its
marvelous prophecies stand completely vindicated.

We could not begin to discuss all these prophecies
here. We shall, however, consider the prophecy of the
70 weeks. Many believe this to be the greatest
prophecy of all. It is found in Daniel 9:24-26:

> Seventy weeks are determined upon thy people
> and upon thy holy city, to finish the transgression,
> and to make an end of sins, and to make reconcili-
> ation for iniquity, and to bring in everlasting
> righteousness, and to seal up the vision and
> prophecy, and to anoint the most Holy.
>
> Know therefore and understand, that from the
> going forth of the commandment to restore and to
> build Jerusalem unto the Messiah the Prince
> shall be seven weeks, and threescore and two
> weeks: the street shall be built again, and the
> wall, even in troublous times [literally "the nar-
> row time," that is, the seven-week period].
>
> And after threescore and two weeks shall Mes-
> siah be cut off, but not for himself [literally "and
> shall have nothing"]: and the people of the prince
> that shall come shall destroy the city and the
> sanctuary; and the end thereof shall be with a

flood [literally "overflow" or "pouring out"], and unto the end of the war desolations are determined [literally "and unto the end, wars and desolations are determined"].

The last week and the doings of "the prince that shall come" (not Messiah) are treated in the 27th verse. This verse seems to refer to events that are yet to come, so we shall not discuss it here.

The word translated "week" in the above prophecy literally means "seven" and is used here to denote a seven-year period. It is the same word as used to denote the seven-year period of the Jewish ordinances, and it becomes evident from a study of the context that seven-year periods are meant by Daniel. However, it is implied in passages in both Genesis and the Revelation that the length of the prophetic year may be the ancient Babylonian lunisolar year of 360 days.

Note then that a period of 49 years of 360 days each was to be spent in rebuilding Jerusalem and 434 more years would elapse until the coming of Messiah the Prince. After that, Messiah would be cut off. The starting point of this period was fixed as the time of the decree to rebuild Jerusalem. When the prophecy was written, of course, the Jews were in captivity in Babylon and their capital city had been destroyed by Nebuchadnezzar.

The decree referred to was most likely the one issued to Nehemiah by Artaxerxes in 445 B.C., a date which has been reasonably well-authenticated in secular history, assuming the standard Ptolemaic chronology to be correct. Even the month and date are noted in the Scriptures. Messiah, then, was to come 483 years after this decree was issued (each year containing 360 days). Allowing for leap years, the date thus obtained is 32 A.D. We cannot enter into the details of this computation here, but Sir Robert Anderson and others have worked it out to the very day and have calculated that on the day indicated by prophecy Christ made his "triumphal entry" into Jerusalem with the multitude singing "Blessed be the King that cometh in the name of the Lord" (Luke 19:38). This was the first time that Christ had permitted the worship and proclamation of himself as Messiah. Later, weeping over his rejection by Jerusalem, he said, "If thou hadst known, even thou, in *this thy day,* the things which belong unto thy peace! but now they are hid from thine eyes" (Luke 19:42).

A week later he was crucified, without receiving the kingdom that was rightfully his: ". . . and Messiah shall be cut off, and shall have nothing." Then a few years later, the Romans completely destroyed Jerusalem and the sanctuary and the Jews were literally "poured out" into their great worldwide dispersion. Furthermore, as the prophecy indicates, there have been "wars and desolations" from that time on, and no doubt these will continue until the end.

Not all scholars agree on this chronology as worked out to the exact day. But Anderson's exposition is convincing and, in any event, the date is remarkably close. Thus the very date of the coming of the Messiah to Jerusalem was set and recorded in the Word of God many hundreds of years before the event. The passages relating to making an end of sins and bringing in everlasting righteousness are not yet fulfilled, but these belong to the final consummation of the 70-week period, and the 70th week has not yet begun. There is a long interval between the completion of the 69th week with the death of Messiah and the beginning of the 70th week.

There are many other prophecies relating to the coming of Christ, possibly not as striking as this, but just as miraculous. His virgin birth was predicted in Isaiah 7:14. His birthplace in Bethlehem was given in Micah 5:2. Zechariah 9:9, 10 describes his public entry into Jerusalem on the foal of an ass. Many details of his teaching and healing ministries are given in various prophecies. His betrayal is described, including even the price of 30 pieces of silver, in Zechariah 11:12, 13. The details of the crucifixion are graphically portrayed in Psalm 22. Psalm 22 was written by David at a time when offenders were killed by stoning and crucifixion—a distinctly Roman method of execution—was unheard of. The purpose of his death, as well as several of the details of his trial, suffering on the cross, and his burial are foretold in Isaiah 53. The fact that he died, not for himself or anything that he had done, but as a substitute for our sins, is stressed as clearly in this passage as anywhere in the New Testament. Even the resurrection is indicated in several places in the Old Testament (e.g., Psalm 16), as well as being foretold several times by Jesus himself.

No one can even begin to explain the hundreds of amazingly fulfilled prophecies in the Bible without admitting the divine authorship of the book. Realizing this, it is more than dangerous to neglect the Scriptures and the Savior presented therein. "For there is none other name under heaven given among men, whereby we must be saved" (Acts 4:12).

There are also many unfulfilled prophecies in the Bible, relating to coming judgment, which people would do well to heed. Just as God is now offering salvation in Christ free to all who will receive it, so he will one day execute judgment upon all who refuse the gift of his love.

"He that believeth on the Son hath everlasting life: and he that believeth not the Son shall not see life; but the wrath of God abideth on him" (John 3:36).

Although we cannot devote a whole chapter to the subject, another important evidence of the inspiration of the Scriptures is contained in the claims and in the very nature and structure of the book itself.

The men who were used to write the Scriptures all claimed that their words were directly from God himself. Such expressions as "God said," "The Lord spake, saying," "The word of the Lord," and similar statements occur 680 times in the Pentateuch, 418 times in the Historical Books, and over 1300 times in the Prophets. The writers of the New Testament quote from the Old 320 times and allude to it hundreds of other times, always using it as the God-inspired Book it claims to be. Incidentally, the Lord Jesus Christ quoted often from the books of Moses and referred to them as such, from Isaiah as written by Isaiah, from Daniel as written by Daniel, and in many ways showed his belief in the full integrity and inspiration of the Scriptures.

As far as the New Testament is concerned, Christ told his apostles that they would be directed later by the Holy Spirit in their speaking and writing (John 14:26; 16:13, 14, etc.). The eight writers of the New Testament books indicate by implication, and often by direct assertion, that their words were guaranteed through their writing under the inspiration of the Holy Spirit. Paul, especially, insisted over and over that his writings were direct revelations from God. Paul's peerless character and devotion to the One for whom he spent and finally gave his life makes absurd the notion of deliberate deception on his part. He says in II Timothy 3:16 that "*All* scripture is given by inspiration of God." Peter says, regarding the Old Testament writers, that "Holy men of God spake as they were moved by the Holy Ghost" (II Peter 1:21). John dares to say, in concluding the Revelation, that anyone taking away from the words of his prophecy would have his part taken from the Book of Life.

If the Bible is not what it claims to be—a direct revelation from God—then the men who wrote it were either the biggest fools or the most colossal liars and frauds that mankind has been disgraced with. How anyone could find mental rest in either of the last two propositions, knowing the incalculable moral and spir-

itual worth and influence of the Bible, knowing something of its miraculous compilation and preservation,
knowing that it is by far the all-time best-seller of the
world, is beyond rational comprehension.

The Bible was written mostly by and about Jews, yet
it is universal in scope. Children love to read or hear
Bible stories, and to memorize many of the precious
promises of God's Word. But also men of the greatest
intellect derive great delight, and mental and spiritual
stimulation, from the study of the Bible. People of all
lands, all occupations, all stations in society, and all
degrees of wealth love the Book.

More than any other book, it speaks with authority
to the universal human conscience, but also with love
and comfort to the heart. It convicts men of their sin
and guilt before a holy God, but also points them to the
Savior, Jesus Christ, whom it reveals.

To one who is willing to go deep into the study of the
Bible, new marvels of plan, of symbol, of structure, of
wording, are continually unfolding themselves.
Though written by approximately 40 authors, in 66
parts, over a period of more than 1,500 years, the Bible
is very definitely one Book, consistent and progressive
in its development and message, every page bearing
witness in some way to the One who is the theme of it
all—the Lord Jesus Christ. There are more than 300
prophecies in the Old Testament concerning the Coming One which were fulfilled at the first appearing of
Christ. Hundreds more in both the Old and New Testaments will be fulfilled at the second coming. In the
Old Testament, there are scores of remarkable types,
or pre-pictures, of Christ, that foretell his career with
such beautiful intimacy and remarkable detail as absolutely to preclude any possibility of coincidence.

Surely, for those who have read thus far, there can
no longer be a reasonable doubt that the Bible is the
literally inspired Word of God. I have not, of course,
even attempted to present an exhaustive study and

refutation of all the difficulties and supposed contradictions and mistakes that 100 generations of
critics have contrived against the Bible. However, I
feel safe in saying that all of them either have already
been answered by conservative scholars, or else can be
answered after prayerful, unprejudiced investigation.
On the other hand, no one can completely understand
and explain the Word of God—that in itself is one of
the proofs that the Bible is the Word of God.

Since such is the case, the significance of the Bible
and its Christ to our personal lives, both here and
hereafter, is inestimably great. Therefore, I suggest
that the reader examine the next chapter carefully and
thoughtfully, even prayerfully, if he has not yet accepted Jesus Christ as the Son of God and his Savior.
Eternal issues are involved in that decision.

THE ETERNAL PLAN OF GOD

7

Of course, no one in this life could even begin to understand anything of the nature of God or his purposes except as he chooses to reveal himself. The mere existence of beauty and goodness in the world and the overwhelming evidences of design in the physical, chemical, and biological realms should suffice to prove to anyone that there exists a great Intelligence or Power behind all things. The fact that men and women, as "effects," have personalities, must mean that the Cause that produced them has a far greater personality. But these facts in themselves cannot reveal the character or intentions of that Being or how people may fulfill the intuitive desire, dormant though it is in many of us, to know him and to identify ourselves more completely with him.

This desire forces them to leave the domain of science and enter the realms of philosophy and theology. Christians, of course, believe that God has given us a supernatural revelation of himself and his plan in the

Bible, and has shown forth his nature and his character in the person of Jesus Christ.

We have examined some of the reasons advanced in support of these claims, and attempted to show that the arguments offered against the inspiration of the Scriptures and the Deity of the Lord Jesus Christ will not stand when examined rationally and without bias. Assuming then that these two premises may be taken as basic, we may hope and expect to find something of God's personality and plan revealed to us on the pages of Scripture and in the character and work of Jesus.

The God thus revealed is, first of all, a personal God, interested tremendously in every living soul. Yet, he is the one "who created heaven . . . and the earth, and the things that therein are" (Rev. 10:6). He has direct power over all the forces of nature; all the laws of the universe were ordained and are enforced by him.

Some people have difficulty with the idea that such infinitesimal entities as men occupying a speck of dust in a remote corner of the universe could be the objects of special solicitude and concern on the part of an infinite God. Yet astronomers have been unable to find real evidence of life as we know it on any other body in the universe. Even though astronomers strongly desire to find evidence of extra-terrestrial life and one of the main purposes of our nation's space program was that very goal, they have been completely unsuccessful in these efforts. It is certain now that life can exist on no other planet in the solar system and there is no observable evidence that any other star in the universe even has a solar system. Even if a few stars do have a system of planets such as the sun has, the chance that one of them would be of the right composition and located at just the right distance from its sun to make life possible is extremely small.

And isn't it true that life and mind, no matter how small the objects in which they are encompassed, are infinitely superior to inanimate objects, no matter how large? The human brain is undoubtedly the most complex aggregation of matter in the universe. Importance and significance are measured by complexity, not by size!

We cannot, of course, understand the whole purpose of God in creating all the stars in the universe. Many of them are very useful, in fact essential, to man in the finding of directions and in the keeping of time. All that are visible to the naked eye are certainly a source of joy and beauty to man. The purpose of those stars that can be seen only through great telescopes can probably never be determined until after Christ's second coming. Then our resurrection bodies, like his, will no longer be subject to the limitations imposed by the gravitational and electromagnetic forces which restrain our present bodies.

The problem of why God created man is of much more immediate and vital concern to us. But even this problem can be but partially and incompletely solved. Certainly there is nothing science has revealed or, in all likelihood, ever can reveal that would throw light on the mystery of life. We have seen how the doctrines of chance and spontaneous generation are little better than absurd. There is most certainly a purpose behind it all but science, unaided by revelation, is completely inadequate and unable to explain that purpose.

But even the Bible gives little information about God's purpose in the creation of life. God has, however, provided ample information in his Word concerning the relation of man, once created, to him and that is the thing that should be of greatest importance to us. It is evident from the Scriptures (note Job 38:4-7), that even before man was created, God had created "an innumerable company of angels" (Hebrews 12:22) for the purpose of being "ministering spirits . . . for them who shall be heirs of salvation" (Hebrews 1:14). It is evident that these beings were not mere automatons but had, like man, the freedom of will and choice. They were glorious creatures but some of them, led by Lucifer (who seems to be identical with Satan) rebelled against God, seeking to overthrow him. However, they were defeated and fell from the high estate God had provided for them. They were not, however, completely destroyed at that time but are still actively working against God's present plan of creation and redemption, being reserved for final destruction at the last great judgment.

There is therefore in the world a very definite source of evil, headed up in the character of Satan, who existed before the creation of man, and who hates and attempts to thwart God and all his plans for mankind. He succeeded in tempting Adam and Eve and bringing about man's fall and God's resultant curse on man and his dominion.

God's work in redeeming fallen man through his Son, Jesus Christ, is in part a demonstration to Satan that God is truly God and that his purposes cannot be set aside by Satan's efforts to become king of the universe. This is only a small part of the truth, however. Many passages in the Bible speak of God's love for man and it is certain that man's creation is somehow an expression of the very nature and heart of God.

It is evident that God is honored by the fellowship and worship of beings made in his own image. It is probably as close to the truth as we can get to say that God made man for fellowship with himself. This fact is indicated by the immeasurable lengths to which he was willing to go to restore that lost fellowship.

The question then arises: "Why did God so constitute man that he was able to reject this fellowship?" The answer, of course, is that true fellowship is voluntary and mutual. Man must have the ability and responsibility to choose or reject God before fellowship with him could mean anything.

Accordingly, God created the first man perfect and put him in a perfect environment, but gave him the power to disobey him if he chose. One simple test was applied—Adam and Eve were not to eat of the tree of the knowledge of good and evil. Everyone is familiar with the record of the temptation of Eve and how she permitted Satan to play upon her pride and desire for wisdom. She yielded to his suggestion and disobeyed God by eating of the forbidden fruit. Adam himself was not deceived, but deliberately sinned by eating the fruit when Eve desired him to.

With Adam's fall, sin entered into the world and the curse of God fell on the earth and on mankind. There are several things involved in the curse. The most significant thing is death. Adam was created to live forever, but God had warned him that death would follow disobedience. All of Adam's descendants, including you and me, have inherited a sin-nature from Adam, and are thus under the curse of God. This sin-nature manifests itself in deliberate acts of sin and disobedience toward God, and it is the universal testimony of men that ". . . all have sinned, and come short of the glory of God" (Romans 3:23). And the universal law of death further testifies that ". . . There is none righteous, no, not one" (Romans 3:10), because God's Word tells us that ". . . the soul that sinneth, it shall die" (Ezekiel 18:4), and ". . . the wages of sin is death" (Romans 6:23). Science has never found an explanation for death; the reason why the cells of the body have the power to reproduce themselves and maintain life for only a certain length of time is completely mysterious. There is no better explanation available than that it is a divine judgment because of sin.

Every physical system, isolated from external sources of energy, must deteriorate until the state of maximum entropy is reached, when all activity must cease and the system is then "dead." Similarly, in the realm of biological life, there is deterioration of the protein compounds throughout the life of the creature, as the more unstable complex molecules give way to simpler, stabler compounds—or as some highly organized organ is injured or diseased, it also deteriorates, until finally biological death ensues.

In an amazingly analogous manner, there is also in the spiritual realm an inexorable law of degeneration. Unless an external source of spiritual and moral energy is somehow granted the individual he will naturally become lower and lower in the scale of morality and spirituality. No matter what a man's outward appearance may seem, or what trappings of religion or culture or ethics he may display, he knows in his heart that his natural inclination is toward that which is lower. If he is to do that which is right, he must discipline himself. If he merely "lets himself go," and yields to his own inmost urges, his God-given conscience rapidly becomes seared, and he quickly falls from his state of outward respectability. Finally, Scripture and experience and conscience all unite in affirming that "sin, when it is finished, bringeth forth death" (James 1:15).

But there is more to death than the mere ending of physical processes. Man was created in the spiritual image of God and thus man's spirit must be eternal in nature, because God is eternal. The body is merely the abode of the spirit.

Since death was instituted as a result of man's deliberate rejection of the conditions upon which the companionship of God depended, it must necessarily include complete separation from God and his love. The spirit is eternal and therefore the judgment of death involves an eternity of complete separation from God, and all that is good. This is called, in Revelation 21:8, the "second death."

I think it probable that everyone who ever lived, regardless of his words of self-justification or his mental assent to any one of a thousand creeds, must have realized in his deepest heart that he, in himself, de-

serves nothing from God but complete rejection. If he
hasn't realized it, he will certainly do so one day when
he comes before the throne of God for judgment. It is
tragically true that most people are so concerned with
their own temporal affairs that any such thoughts or
fears are quickly shunted aside. Many others seem to
think that they are capable in themselves of doing certain things that will please or satisfy God and thus
bribe him into saving them. But the fact remains that
we have all sinned and this fact, in God's sight, makes
us fit only for condemnation. Every one of us has deliberately yielded to sin, and has intentionally and know-
ingly refused to give God first place in our life and
heart. Each one of us deserves nothing from a good and
righteous Creator but eternal spiritual death. In fact,
the very righteousness and justice of God demand it.

Yet, somehow, in spite of man's sin, God still loved
us and desired to have fellowship with us. Even before
God created Adam, he knew that he would fall and
thus bring the penalty of death upon himself and his
seed. And so God had already worked out a plan of
redemption for fallen man, a plan that was complete
and predetermined before the foundation of the world.

God's righteousness demands death and separation
as the penalty for man's sin, but God's mercy sought a
substitute to pay the price in man's stead. But who
would be able to pay the price? It would not be possible
for some man to die for other men, because every man
who had ever lived or would live was a sinner himself
in both nature and practice and thus would have to die
himself for his own sins. Similarly, it seems probable
that the angels had proven themselves incapable of
living without sin apart from the grace of God. None of
them was qualified to act as a substitute for man in
death.

Furthermore, when Adam fell, Satan gained supremacy over the earth. Man, himself, became subject
to the devil. The popular notion of the universal

fatherhood of God is directly contrary to the teachings of the Bible. Consequently, in order to complete the plan of redemption it was necessary not only that the price of sin should be paid, but also that the devil, who held the power of death over mankind, should be defeated. Man's substitute, therefore, had to be able to conquer both Satan and the bonds of death.

No one in the entire universe could meet these qualifications except God himself. But because human redemption required it and because he loved us, God in the fullness of time and in the person of his Son, the second person of the Trinity, took upon himself the form of a man. His name was called Jesus "for he shall save his people from their sins" (Matthew 1:21).

Some people find it difficult to understand why God waited so many thousands of years after man's fall before revealing himself in Christ, and also profess concern for the souls of those millions who lived and died before Christ came. The solution to this problem is not clearly set forth in the Bible for the simple reason that it does not directly concern us today. The Old Testament (especially from Genesis 12 onwards) was written primarily for the Jewish nation before Christ, and the New Testament, together with the Old, for the people of all nations who came after Christ. The way of salvation for these groups is clearly expounded in the Bible. The ancient Jews, it is known from Scripture, were justified by faith in God's promises of deliverance and a future Redeemer; they gave outward evidence of their faith in their sacrifices and offerings, which were ordained by God as symbols or pre-pictures of the one great sacrifice to be offered at Calvary.

They were not saved by the ceremonies or by their works of righteousness, however, but by their faith and trust in God for a means of justification (see Hebrews 11). This also applied to those who were called of God before the beginning of the Hebrew nation, including Abel, Enoch, Noah, Abraham, Isaac and Jacob.

Although we cannot know so definitely, it may be that this was also true of other people of all lands and races. People still retained enough of the divine image, so that they should have been able to realize their need of God and their inadequacy to save themselves. It may be possible that those who did recognize this and who consequently sought God and his will received some sort of revelation from him and were saved. In Hebrews 11:6, we read: "But without faith it is impossible to please him: for he that cometh to God must believe that he is, and that he is a rewarder of them that diligently seek him."

For example, Job was one of the earliest patriarchs and seems to have been unrelated to the Jews or to their ancestors; yet he knew and served God through faith. There are several recorded instances of missionary activity on the part of the Israelites after the Hebrew nation was founded; for example, Jonah preached in Nineveh, with the result that the city repented and turned to the true God.

Even now, there is a marvelous witness to Christ in the heavens, not only in showing forth his power as Creator, but in actually testifying to his atoning death, his glorious resurrection, and his coming again. The constellations, which have existed from before recorded history much in their present form, were (according to Genesis 1:14; Job 9:9; 26:13; 38:31, and other references) established by God as "signs" to serve, perhaps, as a primitive revelation of himself and his plan and to "declare the Glory of God" (the "Glory of God" is Christ—see Psalm 19).

These astral signs seem to tell, in symbolic form, the story of the coming divine, virgin-born "Seed of the woman," who was to bruise the Serpent's head (Genesis 3:15). They show his death on the cross as God's offering for the sins of lost mankind, his formation of the Church as his Body and his Bride, and his second coming to consummate his work in the complete destruction of the Serpent and sin.

This original, evangelic presentation of Christ was, and is, available to all tribes and tongues, if rightly understood. However, man has corrupted it into pagan mythology and astrology. These have been turning men away from Christ, rather than to him. The same is true to some degree of most ancient myths and legends, which reflect primeval history and revelation grossly distorted and corrupted by pagan philosophy and occultism.

It seems that most of the ancients were not concerned with faith in the one true God, but yielded their lives and souls to the power of the flesh and the devil. The antediluvians were so wicked that God spared only eight people out of the millions or even billions who were destroyed by the flood. Only Lot and his daughters were found righteous in the cities of Sodom and Gomorrah. God ordered the Israelites to cut off whole cities and nations because of their wickedness and idolatry. It is very doubtful whether even a direct revelation from God to these peoples would have mattered very much to them.

But I believe that, if there were any who did sincerely desire to find God and to renew the lost fellowship with him, then he did reveal himself to them somehow. Perhaps this is true even of anyone who, though having come after Christ, has never heard of him and yet diligently sought God in faith. This is not to imply that the various non-Christian religions of the world and the numerous pseudo-Christian sects in Christendom offer alternate ways to God.

The Bible, including Christ's own teaching on the subject, is very definite in teaching that salvation is only through the sacrificial death of Christ, and that it is granted freely to all who receive it on this basis. All religions except biblical Christianity teach, on the other hand, that salvation depends in a greater or lesser part on the works of man. They cater to man's pride, while God desires man's love and gratitude rendered in response to his free gift of salvation made available by his own infinite suffering.

If men such as we are speaking of, not having an opportunity to hear the Gospel of Christ, are to come to God at all, it cannot be on the basis of their particular religion. It must rather be on the basis of the work of Christ (even if they have not heard of that work) in his atoning death for the sins of the world. They must, with real sincerity, believe in God and desire to know him. Also, they must recognize their own sinfulness and inability to please God, and believe that God will somehow provide the means whereby their sin can be forgiven. They must respond in faith to whatever true light (note John 1:9) from God they may have received (in nature, by conscience or through primeval revelation).

This, in all essentials, is the attitude of mind and heart that any person takes when becoming a Christian. He is saved on the basis of Christ's work on the cross and through his own attitude of repentance and faith toward God in Christ. The only difference is that one has been given knowledge of the work of Christ as the basis of salvation and the other has not. Since salvation is by grace through faith, it may be reasonable to believe that God can, on such a basis as outlined above, provide salvation for one who has not yet had the opportunity to hear of the Lord Jesus.

It then should be also evident that if there are such people who have been saved in this way, they will gladly acknowledge Christ as Savior when later they do learn of him. When such a person hears of him, he then will have found the way to God which he had sought, and the witness of the Holy Spirit in his heart will assure him of this and of his own salvation. The experience of Cornelius (Acts 10, especially verses 34-35) is a good case in point.

But this hypothetical possibility can most certainly not be legitimately used as excuse for indifference toward Christian missionary effort. Rather, the hope of finding those whose hearts are right toward God and anxious to learn more fully of him should be added incentive for missions. In addition, it should be clear that few, if any, would ever be saved in the way indicated above, but that, with the full light of the Gospel of Christ presented by missionaries, many, many more will be saved as they turn from darkness to the light, receiving Christ as their Savior.

However interested we may be in such speculations about those who do not ever hear the Gospel, we ourselves know of Jesus Christ and His work.

Jesus, as a man, lived the only sinless human life since the foundation of the world. This was the testimony of even his enemies, whose only charge against him was that he claimed to be God. He was not even born with a sin-nature, because he was not conceived according to the flesh but by the Holy Spirit, and was born of a virgin. Consequently he alone was qualified to suffer God's judgment of death as a substitute for others.

Jesus Christ was able to perform miracles and to teach men with divine authority God's way of life for those in his kingdom. Furthermore, he was able to conquer Satan and his power of death.

He, bearing the sins of the whole world, died on the cross of Calvary and, for one awful interval, suffered the agony of complete separation from the fellowship of God the Father—the second death. With the spirit departed from the physical body, he somehow broke the bonds of death and Satan. When he returned, he could say: "I am he that liveth, and was dead; and, behold, I am alive for evermore, Amen; and have the keys of hell and of death" (Revelation 1:18).

He rose from the grave on the third day and soon after returned into the heavens. God's plan of redemp-

tion was complete. The death and resurrection of Jesus
Christ are sufficient in God's sight to atone for the sin
of the whole world, and to completely restore lost mankind into the fellowship of God. It is on this basis alone
that God can or will bring forgiveness and salvation to
lost humanity.

But God still will not force anyone to come to himself against that person's will. God has provided the
way but each individual must accept it and appropriate it for himself. If anyone so chooses, he is perfectly
free to reject all that God has done and all that He
offers—free to go on living under the power of the
world and the flesh and the devil, subject to eternal
separation from God in the second death.

It would seem that no one in his right mind could
reject God's offer of mercy in Christ Jesus. To avail
oneself of the immeasurable blessing made available,
nothing whatsoever is required except a simple acceptance of the Lord Jesus Christ as personal Savior:

Believe on the Lord Jesus Christ, and thou shalt
be saved (Acts 16:31).

That if thou shalt confess with thy mouth the Lord
Jesus, and shalt believe in thine heart that God
hath raised him from the dead, thou shalt be
saved (Romans 10:9).

He that heareth my word, and believeth on him
that sent me, hath everlasting life, and shall not
come into condemnation; but is passed from death
unto life (John 5:24).

That whosoever believeth in him should not
perish, but have eternal life (John 3:15).

Neither is there salvation in any other: for there

is none other name under heaven given among
men, whereby we must be saved (Acts 4:12).

But, amazing though it is, it is true that the masses
of people still reject Christ and refuse to accept God's
matchless gift of his only begotten Son. I cannot agree
with those people who maintain that a just God could
not send anyone into eternal punishment. There is no
imaginable punishment that could adequately com-
pensate for a knowing and deliberate rejection of the
sinless Son of God who willingly and lovingly died for
our sins.

The Scriptures teach, incidentally, that those who
know of Christ and reject him will be subjected to a
greater degree of punishment than those unsaved men
who never hear the Gospel (see Luke 12:42-48).

Those who do believe in the Lord Jesus Christ, however, and entrust their souls to him, are saved and are
born again by the Holy Spirit. Each believing soul becomes immediately "a new creature" (II Corinthians
5:17) in Christ Jesus and a part of the Body of Christ.
"But as many as received him, to them gave he power
to become the sons of God, even to them that believe on
his name" (John 1:12). Baptism or church membership
or good works do not provide—or even help provide—
salvation. It is true that real conversion produces a
changed nature in the believer which desires to obey
all the teachings and ordinances of Christ—and these
most certainly do include baptism, church membership, and good works—but the genuine Christian does
these things *because* he is saved, not to obtain salvation.

It is, of course, painfully true that many who profess
to be Christians live in the worldly manner of those
who are not Christians. Probably many of these have
never experienced true regeneration and their lives
have, consequently, not been changed. On the other
hand, since the old nature is still present to a certain

extent even with the true Christian and will be until his redemption is one day completed in resurrection and glorification, it continually manifests itself in his life and acts, to an extent depending inversely on his degree of commitment to Christ and his service. But even though the born-again man continues to commit acts of sin against God daily, the Holy Spirit within him makes his nature tend to abhor sin and love the ways of God. This change in inner attitude reveals itself in a changed life and manner of conduct. If the skeptic is honest, he must admit that the great majority of real Christian men and women live on a much higher spiritual and moral plane than those who are unsaved.

While it is true that salvation is only by "grace through faith," the Bible does teach that there will be a difference in the matter of reward for Christians. This depends on their faithfulness and service in living according to the will of Christ and in doing whatever they can to spread the message of salvation. However, the one great and outstanding certainty is that those who accept and believe in the person and finished work of the Lord Jesus Christ will enjoy the blessed fellowship of God throughout all eternity; those who reject Christ must suffer complete and eternal separation from God.

The question of predestination bothers many people. It is certainly taught in the Bible that God, being both omnipotent and omniscient, knows and controls all things that will ever happen, and, in fact, just who will accept Christ and who will reject him. In some way we cannot understand, those who would accept Christ were elected or chosen, then predestinated and finally called (See Romans 8:28-31; I Peter 1:2, 20; Ephesians 1:3-12, etc.). The implication, however, is not that God arbitrarily or capriciously picks out certain individuals to justify and certain others to condemn. It is part of the plan of God that each person should have the freedom and responsibility to accept or reject God's provision for restoration of lost fellowship. It is folly for an individual to refuse to do anything about accepting Christ, or for Christians to refuse to undertake evangelism or to sponsor mission work on the ground that God will see to it that those who are predestinated to be saved will be saved and that those who are not called will not be saved.

In God's sight, it is true that those who will accept Christ are foreknown and foreordained. But since we cannot know or understand the mind of God, we cannot understand the doctrine of predestination, even though it is wonderful for those who are Christians to realize that they have been known and loved of God since the world began. "All things work together for good to them that love God, to them who are the called according to his purpose" (Romans 8:28).

On the other hand, there is no clearer teaching in the Bible than that the death of Christ was sufficient to atone for the sin of the whole world; that each person has complete freedom to appropriate the work of the Lord Jesus Christ to himself if he will only do so; and that each individual is completely responsible for the results of his sin if he rejects Christ.

We may not be able to understand how predestination and free will can exist together in the same person; neither can we understand how God can be three persons and yet be one God; neither can we understand how both God and man could have been together in the person of Jesus Christ; nor, for that matter, can we understand very much of the mystery of creation or of the deeper significance of the atonement. There is much in the Word of God and in his plan that our human minds cannot grasp. One day, I believe, the Lord Jesus will open up all these mysteries to us when we are with him in glory. But now, the greatest and most urgent matter before every man or woman is the question: "What will you do with the Lord Jesus? The responsibility is yours. If you accept him, he will give you everlasting life, and will make you a child of God in him. If you refuse him and his love and his death for you, you have no hope of ever, in all eternity, finding God. What will you do with Jesus?" And to every Christian, the Scriptures clearly teach that the most important job he has is to do all he can to give others the story of salvation and, by God's grace, to lead them to the Lord Jesus Christ.

If you are expecting to find salvation and peace through reason, or through good character and morals, or through church membership, or through certain sacraments and rituals, or through philosophy, or through anything other than the blood of Jesus Christ, you are certain to fail. You must come in the one way God has provided if you come at all. The Lord Jesus said: "I am the way, the truth, and the life: no man cometh unto the Father, but by me" (John 14:6). Only one way, yet that way is open to all and is available for the taking.

If you sincerely desire to be saved, to accept the Lord Jesus Christ as your personal Savior, all that is necessary is for you to confess your need of a Savior and trust in the Lord Jesus Christ to save you. Belief in him will obtain for you the assurance of sins forgiven and of salvation and eternal life, on the authority of the Word of God.

Millions of Christians down through the ages have proven by their lives and often by their deaths that the saving power of Christ is wholly genuine. There are millions of men and women living today whose veracity is unquestioned by even the most vindictive enemies of Christianity. These would say with Paul: "I know whom I have believed, and am persuaded that he is able to keep that which I have committed unto him against that day" (II Timothy 1:12).

Salvation, of course, involves much more than a changed heart and manner of living during the present

life. Important as is the method of living this life, the
sure and certain hope of the Christian for the life to
come is even more important. The Bible does not go
into details as to what we can expect in heaven; in fact,
it is probably impossible for mortal minds to understand very much of it. One thing we can know, however; we have eternal life with Christ. Nothing in the
universe can take that away from us if we have truly
received him as our Savior. He said: "My sheep hear
my voice, and I know them, and they follow me: And I
give unto them eternal life; and they shall never
perish, neither shall any man pluck them out of my
hand" (John 10:27,28). Paul said: "For I am persuaded,
that neither death, nor life, nor angels, nor prin-
cipalities, nor powers, nor things present, nor things to
come, nor height, nor depth, nor any other creature,
shall be able to separate us from the love of God, which
is in Christ Jesus our Lord" (Romans 8:38,39).

Beyond the unending personal nearness of Christ, it
is impossible for us to understand much of what is in
store for us. But it will consist of the greatest and most
wonderful blessings that the infinite love of God can
conceive; we can be sure of that. I am content to wait
until that day to discover the surprises God has in
store for us. The main thing is that my Savior will be
there and that is more than sufficient to satisfy all the
desires of my soul.

One of the ways we can know we have fellowship
with God when we accept Christ is through answered
prayer. The atheists and deists and pantheists and all
others who scoff at the notion of a God who hears and
answers prayer deserve nothing but pity. Every real
Christian knows beyond all question that God does answer prayer. If the time and space were available, I
could tell of one instance after another of marvelous
answers to prayer in my own life and experience, many
of them little short of miraculous.

Until a person becomes a Christian, he can know

nothing of the "unsearchable riches of Christ." As Paul says: ". . .the natural man receiveth not the things of the Spirit of God: for they are foolishness unto him: neither can he know them, because they are spiritually discerned" (I Corinthians 2:14). Even one who has accepted Christ but who is living on much the same plane as before receiving him does not begin to know the joys of the Christian life. Although my own life has been far from what it should have been, I have experienced enough of it to be able to testify unreservedly to the magnificent reality of salvation in Christ and fellowship with God through him.

When I was writing the first edition of this book in 1945, I had only been a convinced and committed Christian about four or five years, and most of my life and career were ahead of me. I was 27 years old and the father of two small children. I was an instructor with a B.S. degree and had never written a book before. This second edition is being prepared 32 years later, and the greater part of my life is behind me. We now have six grown and married children, plus five grandchildren. I have spent the intervening years teaching in six colleges or universities and have published 25 books since that first one. It may add something to say that the experience of these three intervening decades necessitated no changes in the testimony on the preceding pages.

My wife, Mary Louise, and I can now add the further testimony that God's promises in Scripture have been abundantly verified in our lives through all the years and up to this very day. All of our children, for example, have become solid and fruitful Christians, loving each other, loving their parents, loving the Lord! Every financial and physical need has been supplied, and his spiritual blessings over the years have been incalculable. We have seen God do "great and mighty things" (Jeremiah 33:3) which we could never even have thought about 32 years ago. I believe more firmly than ever that "thy word is true from the beginning: and every one of thy righteous judgments endureth for ever" (Psalm 119:160). The final paragraph of this chapter—just below—is exactly the same as when it was first written many years ago, and the testimony is even more sure today.

Reader, in the words of John's Gospel, may I explain my one reason for writing this book. "But these are written, that ye might believe that Jesus is the Christ, the Son of God; and that believing ye might have life through his name" (John 20:31).

THE SIGNS
OF THE TIMES

8

In Chapter Six, a number of the Bible's fulfilled prophecies were pointed out. These fulfillments are too numerous and too remarkably accurate to admit of coincidence. Consequently, it seems a great mistake to neglect the great host of prophecies whose fulfillment belongs to the time of the end. Many of these predictions are coming true in these days, a fact which is responsible for the quickening of the hope in Bible-believing Christians that the Lord Jesus Christ will return soon. Then, too, these events afford present-day, visual proof of the fact of fulfilled prophecy and the truth of the Scriptures.

First, however, a word of caution is necessary against the temptation to set dates or to take passages of Scripture out of their proper context and natural meaning, as some writers on biblical prophecy have done. It is clearly stated in the Bible that the exact time of Christ's return cannot be foreknown by men. We should always be watching for him and living in the light of his imminent return. Furthermore, all the passages that deal with these signs of the last days are intended primarily for encouragement and exhortation, not for the satisfaction of sensationalistic curiosity.

There are differences of interpretation of the prophetic themes of Scripture, even among people who are sincere, born-again, Bible-believing Christians. All Christians, however, agree in the essential of the blessed hope, namely, that Jesus Christ will some day return to this earth, and that it is he who will eventually judge the world in righteousness.

Though some would disagree, I personally believe the Bible indicates that many other events of great importance will take place on the earth, in connection with Christ's return, including the world's greatest outburst of godlessness before he comes and his millennial reign of righteousness afterwards. Also, I believe the Bible teaches that his return will occupy a period of time (just as did his first coming), and that it will involve two main stages—the first to receive those who are saved, the second to judge the nations—and that many of the prophetic Scriptures deal with the period between these two stages of his coming. Finally, all Bible-believing Christians agree that God will eventually create new heavens and a new earth, where those who are saved will live eternally with their God and Savior.

For the purposes of this chapter, the exact outline of the prophetic future is secondary; that which is primary is the fact that *Christ is coming again, and that there are many biblical indications that his return may be very soon!* We shall, therefore, briefly consider a few of these signs.

In Matthew 24:3, the disciples asked Jesus: "What shall be the sign of thy coming, and of the end of the world?" Instead of rebuking them and saying it was none of their business, Jesus proceeded to give them the sign they asked for. He first told them, however, that ordinary wars and rumors of wars would not constitute the sign. "For, he said (and this is the sign), "nation shall rise against nation, and kingdom against kingdom: and there shall be famines, and pestilences, and earthquakes, in divers places" (Matthew 24:7).

The idiom employed here connotes a worldwide state of war, associated with famines, pestilences, and earthquakes. Although it is true that wars have continued through all the centuries of human history, and there have always been famines and pestilences, it is significant that there had never been a real world war until the great conflict of 1914-18, and that the world's greatest famines, pestilences, and earthquakes of all time accompanied and followed it. Jesus said that "these are the beginning of sorrows" (or, more literally, "the first birth-pains").

The destruction and economic chaos following this war caused tremendous famines in many parts of the world, especially in China and Russia, where literally many tens of millions of people starved to death. The great depression of the years after 1930 was also an outgrowth of this war. The world's greatest pestilence of all time, the great influenza epidemic, also accompanied the war. One-third of the world's population was stricken, with probably 15,000,000 people perishing as a result. Finally, the two most catastrophic recorded earthquakes of all time occurred in China in 1920 and in Japan in 1923, in each of which hundreds of thousands were killed.

Two decades after this "first birth-pang" came the second great world war, greater still in intensity and destructiveness, and in its wake, unimaginable horrors of starvation and disease. Also, one cannot help but notice the frequency with which reports come in these days of severe earthquakes occurring "in divers places."

Following World War II have been almost continuous local wars in various parts of the world—the Chinese revolution, the Communist takeover of much of Europe and Asia, the Korean War, the Indo-China War, military takeovers in various South American, African, Asian and European nations, the Vietnamese Conflict, the Arab-Israeli Wars, wars in Angola, Sudan, Cambodia, India, Pakistan, Cyprus, Algeria, and others, not to mention racial conflicts just about everywhere. Though no World War III has yet been activated, it would not take much to start it.

Furthermore, despite scientific advances and political economics, famines, pestilences and earthquakes continue to take great tolls every year. Surely it is significant that these four great signs have been occurring simultaneously on the greatest scale in history since the days of World War I.

Speaking of the second coming, Jesus also said: "And as it was in the days of Noah, so shall it be also in the days of the Son of man" (Luke 17:26). Regarding the days of Noah, we read in Genesis 6:5 and 11:". . .the wickedness of man was great in the earth. . .The earth also was corrupt before God, and the earth was filled with violence." Today, there is more crime, more corruption, more drunkenness, more vice, more violence, than the world has ever seen since the days of Noah. Even more serious is the universal relaxation of moral and religious principles. Whole nations have turned gangster and murderer. Jesus must have been speaking of our day; there has never been a time that so aptly fits His description. Other characteristics of the days of Noah, duplicated in our day, seem to have been indifference to the things of God, great advances in the arts and sciences, and disregard of God's primal law of permanent and monogamous marriage.

II Timothy 3:1-5 gives a more detailed account of the moral conditions that were to be prevalent in the world in the last times:

This know also, that in the last days perilous times shall come. For men shall be lovers of their own selves, covetous, boasters, proud, blasphemers, disobedient to parents, unthankful, unholy, without natural affection, trucebreakers, false accusers, incontinent, fierce, despisers of those that are good, traitors, heady, high-minded, lovers of pleasures more than lovers of God; having a form of godliness, but denying the power thereof.

If the above adjectives are examined in turn, it will quickly be noted how remarkably well they describe most of the people in the world today. Although there have been individuals meriting such descriptions during all ages, the proportions have never been so great as today.

Widespread tensions and conflicts between capital and labor are prophesied in the fifth chapter of James as typical of the last days:

Go to now, ye rich men, weep and howl for your miseries that shall come upon you. Your riches are corrupted, and your garments are moth-eaten. Your gold and silver is cankered; and the rust of them shall be a witness against you, and shall eat your flesh as it were fire. Ye have heaped treasure together for the *last days*. Behold, the hire of the laborers who have reaped down your fields, which is of you kept back by fraud, crieth: and the cries of them which have reaped are entered into the ears of the Lord of Sabaoth. Ye have lived in pleasure on the earth, and been wanton; ye have nourished your hearts, as in a day of slaughter.

This is a vivid description of the way that many of the big landowners and other rich men of the world in recent decades have used the laboring classes as a means to gain fabulous wealth, only to use it wastefully and wantonly. There is little doubt that the majority of the world's rich people (although not all of them, by any means) have gained and used their wealth in the manner indicated here by James. As a result, the common people of all countries have been rising up against the rich. In some countries, this has produced revolution and anarchy, followed by Communism and Fascism. In the United States, it has become only an intense struggle between capital and the labor unions. In many nations, the rich men of the world are indeed "weeping and howling for the miseries that are come upon them." Political and labor leaders have in many places corrupted the labor movements, and to some degree a small number of the ultra-rich have managed to turn even these to their own economic advantage. The trigger that started and fueled these conflicts and revolutions, however, was the fraudulent exploitation of labor by the capitalists, just as James had said it would.

One of the most important signs of the times is the great apostasy that has come upon Christendom. In II Thessalonians 2:3, we read: ". . .that day [the day when Christ shall return; see the context] shall not come, except there come a falling away first." The word translated "falling away" is the Greek word from which our word "apostasy" is obtained, so this verse may well refer to a falling away from the fundamental and basic doctrines. Religious liberals may not like to be called apostates, but the question of the correctness of their teachings notwithstanding, they have abandoned the basic and traditional tenets of Christianity, and consequently *are* apostates, because that is what the word means. The above quotation from II Timothy, ". . .Having a form of godliness, but denying the power thereof" (II Timothy 3:5) is a terse description of liberalism, which seeks to explain away all the supernatural in Christianity. A number of other passages from the Bible might be quoted that also indicate that

the professing Church as a whole will have fallen away
from the New Testament faith at the time of the return
of Christ.

The apostasy is evident not only in liberal churches,
but may be regarded as applying to entire nations.
Germany, Russia, France, Sweden and Denmark,
among many others, were once at least nominally
Christian but now are almost entirely anti-Christian.
There is no country on earth, in fact, that can be regarded as Christian in the biblical sense of the word. In
the United States it is a fact, supported by statistics,
that the great majority of its intellectuals and political
leaders, possibly as much as 75 percent, no longer believe in such supposedly outmoded doctrines as the
verbal inspiration of the Bible, the creation and fall of
man, the virgin birth, the vicarious nature of Christ's
death on the cross, the resurrection and ascension, or,
for that matter, anything partaking of the miraculous
or supernatural. This is also true of most of the seminary professors, pastors and other religious leaders in
most of the main-line Christian denominations today.
Without these things, Christianity is only a social re-
form movement, with absolutely nothing to satisfy the
individual need for God. It is certainly not the Christianity of the Bible.

Tragic as all this may be, it is connected in the Scriptures with the last days and is therefore intensely significant to the believer and a soleman warning to those
outside of Christ.

Another latter-day development in the realm of religion is indicated in I Timothy 4:1-3. "Now the Spirit
speaketh expressly, that in the latter times some shall
depart from the faith, giving heed to seducing spirits,
and doctrines of devils [literally "demons"]; speaking
lies in hypocrisy; having their conscience seared with a
hot iron; forbidding to marry, and commanding to ab-
stain from meats. . ."

Occultism and mysticism have, of course, flourished

since the dawn of history. Idol worship, which, as the Bible teaches, is in reality demon or devil worship, has always been attended by magic, soothsaying, spirit-talking, healings, and other strange phenomena, as well as by grossly immoral rites and ceremonies. The student and believer of Scripture knows that all this stems directly from the influence—sometimes known, sometimes unknown—of the hosts of Satan, the demons.

However, it is only within the past hundred years, that these things have reappeared in Christian lands. The tremendous rise of Spiritism, Theosophy, Buddhism, and the scores of smaller cults and "doctrines of devils" that are flooding our land today, certainly point to an intensified activity of the powers of Satan. Add to these the hordes of astrologists, fortune-tellers, palmists, mind-readers, and other occultists that are exerting such an enormous influence over millions of people and it seems almost certain that Paul's prophecy is being fulfilled today. Incidentally, it is most interesting that one of the greatest centers of Spiritism and its kindred evils in America, for the past generation, has been Washington, D.C.

It is also significant that two of the most prominent doctrines of the more sinister of these cults (Theosophy, Spiritism, Buddhism, Hinduism, and other eastern religions currently invading once-Christian nations) are abstinence from meats and marriage. Even more important is their absolute denial of the Lord Jesus Christ and his substitutionary death, and their teaching that salvation can be obtained only through works and individual punishment for sins. This teaching is invariably a mark of anti-Christian doctrine, whether in supernaturalistic or materialistic circles (see I John 2:21-23; 4:1-3).

Along with the great apostasy, there is a smaller trend evident in the circle of real Christians—a renewed and revived interest in the second coming of

Christ. This was to be expected and was prophesied to take place during the last days. Symbolically, it may be represented by the great shout: "Behold the bridegroom cometh!" in the parable of the ten virgins in Matthew 25.

For the most part, however, this hope has been ridiculed even by the majority of Christians. This was also anticipated in that marvelous third chapter of Peter's second epistle, verses 3 through 6:

> Knowing this first, that there shall come in the last days scoffers, walking after their own lusts, and saying, Where is the promise of his coming? for since the fathers fell asleep, all things continue as they were from the beginning of the creation. For this they willingly are ignorant of, that by the word of God the heavens were of old, and the earth standing out of the water and in the water: Whereby the world that then was, being overflowed with water, perished.

Peter also foretold that the basis for their denial of the future intervention of God in his creation would be their denial of the very fact of creation itself. The statement that ". . .all things continue as they were from the beginning of the creation" is very significant. It is the most succinct and yet most complete statement of the doctrine of evolutionary uniformitarianism I have ever seen. It states that all phenomena that we know now are explainable in terms of laws and forces that are now operating and, in fact, have always been operating. Even creation is not recognized as something distinct and complete. These forces are not said to have been operating just since the end of creation, but since the *beginning* of creation. In other words, creation itself was nothing different from what is now taking place—creation is still going on, and is consequently being accomplished by perfectly

natural laws. No event of an unnatural or supernatural nature has ever taken place, and thus there
has never been any real special creation at all. Consequently, even Jesus Christ is the product of evolution, and could not have risen from the dead. It is
foolish therefore to think that he is going to come
again from heaven. "Where is the promise of his coming?"

This is exactly what evolutionists, rationalists,
humanists, atheists, and all the rest have been teaching for at least the past century. This is the doctrine
that is responsible for the tremendous decline in spiritual and moral values in the world; this is the teaching
that has given birth to Communism, Fascism, Nazism,
and anarchism. This philosophy of evolution and materialism has already generated two world wars. And
it is described in the Bible as being the scientific attitude that will prevail on the earth in the last days.

Furthermore, as has been shown in the third and
fourth chapters, the scientific basis of the entire theory
is the deliberate and knowing denial of the overwhelming evidence for special creation and the reality of
judgment through a world-destroying Flood only a few
thousand years ago. The prophecy also indicates this:
"For this they *willingly* are ignorant of, that by the
word of God the heavens were of old, and the earth
standing out of the water and in the water: Whereby
the world that then was, being overflowed with water,
perished." (II Peter 3:5, 6) Truly, this is one of the most
remarkable prophecies in the Bible, and is itself proof
of the inspiration of the Scriptures.

There is another important passage in the 24th
chapter of Matthew, in addition to the one we have
already discussed. Jesus is still speaking of the events
of the end-time and says (verses 32-34):

Now learn a parable of the fig tree; When his
branch is yet tender, and putteth forth leaves, ye

know that summer is nigh: So likewise ye, when ye
shall see all these things, know that it is near,
even at the doors. Verily I say unto you, This generation shall not pass, till all these things be fulfilled.

Obviously, the fig tree is a symbol. The parable was
hardly necessary to emphasize the signs that Jesus
had already discussed (the world war, earthquakes,
famines and pestilences). In Scripture, the fig tree is
often a picture of Judah and the vine or vineyard one of
all Israel. Texts that corroborate this are Joel 1:6,7;
Jeremiah 24:5-8; Isaiah 5:1-7; and Luke 13:6-9, among
others.

Therefore, the parable evidently means that Judah
and its capital Jerusalem will begin to revive near the
time of the second coming. The fig tree was destined to
be barren and unfruitful for some 1,900 years, but
Jesus said it would blossom again. This same recovery,
and also the return of many Jews from the great dispersion near the time of the end, was also predicted by
Moses and many of the Old Testament prophets. See,
for example, such prophecies as Ezekiel 36:24; 37:21;
Jeremiah 23:7,8; 30:3; and many others.

This very thing is now taking place, although 75
years ago it would have seemed absolutely unthinkable. In 1867, there were fewer than 10,000 Jews in all
Palestine, and the land, inhabited almost entirely by
Arabs, was little better than a desert. The modern
Zionist movement was begun in 1897, however, and
the famous Balfour Declaration made in 1917. Later in
the same year, Jerusalem was taken from the Turks by
the British under General Allenby. The Turks did not
even offer any resistance because of a Mohammedan
tradition that, when a man named Prophet-of-God
(Allah-bey) entered Jerusalem, then that city must go
back to the Jews.

Under the banners of Zionism and the Palestine Restoration Movement, great numbers of Jews returned to their traditional home. Swamps and deserts were transformed into cultivated fields and modern cities. Airports, harbors, universities, factories, have been built. The Hebrew language has been revived, and the "former and latter rains," which were absent from the land for so long, returned. The great wealth of world Jewry has aided in the transformation, as predicted in Jeremiah 32:37,43,44. The Dead Sea minerals, estimated to be worth over one trillion dollars, are being taken from the sea in abundance, also in accordance with prophecy. The city of Haifa is now a great seaport and the terminus of a large oil pipeline, things which were predicted. The city of Jerusalem now exceeds the boundaries predicted in Jeremiah 31:38-40 and Zechariah 14:10, although the city until modern times had never extended anywhere near these bounds. In all, there are now over 3,000,000 Jews in Palestine and millions more are anxious to go there.

Perhaps the most significant event of all in this connection is the actual formation of the nation Israel, and its recognition in 1948 by the other nations of the world. Bible scholars, on the basis of God's Word, foretold this a century and more ago, when as yet such an eventuality seemed quite impossible.

Jesus, predicting God's judgment on Jerusalem because of her rejection of him, her Messiah, said: "Jerusalem shall be trodden down of the Gentiles, until the times of the Gentiles be fulfilled" (Luke 21:24). This prophecy has continued unbroken for 1,950 years, and Jerusalem is still trodden down of the Gentiles. But Jesus also implied that some day Jerusalem would no longer belong to Gentiles, and that in that day the "times of the Gentiles" would be finished. This phrase almost certainly points to the great mass of Scripture teaching a Messianic rule over the whole earth, centered in Israel, following the personal return of Jesus

Christ, and Israel's national recognition of him as her Messiah and Savior.

In the Six-Day War, Israel took the old city of Jerusalem back from the Arabs and has controlled it ever since—*with one exception*. The Arabs still control the spot on which the great Temple stood, since their sacred Dome-of-the-Rock Mosque now occupies that site. The Israelis have been unable or unwilling to take it away from them. Since the Temple is, in God's estimation, synonymous with Jerusalem, this means that Biblical Jerusalem is still "trodden down of the Gentiles," and Luke 21:24 is still awaiting its fulfillment.

Jesus said that he would be "even at the doors" (Matthew 24:33) when these things "begin to come to pass" (Luke 21:28). He also said "This generation shall not pass, till all these things be fulfilled" (Matthew 24:34). He was saying here that his coming in power and glory, together with all the notable events he had just mentioned as preceding it, would all be fulfilled before a certain generation had passed away—"this" generation. The word is correctly translated here as "generation" (Some have thought that it meant the Jewish "race"—which word, however, is slightly different in the Greek from that for "generation."), and seems most obviously to refer to the generation that "sees these things." The phrase "this generation" could quite as well be translated "that generation," since the Greek adjective is demonstrative.

In other words, the generation that sees the sign of the first great birth-pang, the predicted World War with its associated famines, pestilences, and earthquakes—that sees, especially, the fig tree, Israel, budding—*that* generation shall not pass away until all these other things are fulfilled.

This seems almost undoubtedly to mean our generation! How this ought to thrill us as we anticipate meeting soon our wonderful Lord face to face! But in John's words, how urgently important it is that we "abide in him; that, when he shall appear, we may have confidence, and not be ashamed before him at his coming"! (I John 2:28).

There is another very significant development peculiar to our generation. That is, the very principle by which God may intend to purge the world at the time of the coming of Christ in glory seems to have been discovered by man when atomic energy was released in all its enormous power. In II Peter 3:10-12, the Holy Spirit inspired the following words:

> But the day of the Lord will come as a thief in the night; in the which the heavens shall pass away with a great noise, and the elements shall melt with fervent heat, the earth also and the works that are therein shall be burned up. Seeing then that all these things shall be dissolved, what manner of persons ought ye to be in all holy conversation and godliness, Looking for and hasting unto the coming of the day of God, wherein the heavens being on fire shall be dissolved, and the elements shall melt with fervent heat?

Note the words, "elements," "fervent heat," "dissolved," "great noise," "burned up." Enough has been written on the subject of atomic energy and the terrifying potential of the atomic bomb in particular for anyone to note immediately the implications of the above passage.

Atoms, of course, are known by us as "elements," and our understanding of the word is supported fully by the Greek from which the above translation was made, the word being understood to mean the fundamental components of matter. The entire passage seems to describe what might happen to the earth and its environs if nuclear warfare should happen to develop. This is an eventuality which is not at all impossible and which is greatly feared by both scientist and layman. Jesus' prophecy of the last days in Luke

21:25,26 is certainly being experienced today—"Upon the earth distress of nations, with perplexity. . .men's hearts failing them for fear, and for looking after those things which are coming on the earth: for the powers of heaven shall be shaken."

Regardless of the time for the eventual fulfillment of the above passages, these modern discoveries and present conditions impart to them real timeliness. I cannot see how any person today can not be distressed and perplexed and fearful about those things coming on the earth unless he knows Christ as his Savior. "Yet once more," says the Lord in Hebrews 12:26,27,29, "I shake not the earth only, but also heaven. . .that those things which cannot be shaken may remain. . . .For our God is a consuming fire."

Most of these signs of the nearing end of the age are indicative of an appalling state of things. No hope is offered of a better world, or of either national or individual growth in morality and righteousness. The picture presented is of a society in which there will be great wars, much disease and hunger, frequent convulsions of nature, intense class struggle, racial and religious hatreds, ever-lowering moral and ethical standards, widespread religious apostasy, evidences of increasing demonic activity, a prevalent philosophy of materialism and naturalism, widespread confusion and fear of things to come—a society in which, according to Daniel 12:4, knowledge and technology will be much advanced, but which is nevertheless ripe for judgment.

In the midst of such a world situation, one of the very few bright spots is the amazing rebirth of the Jewish nation. Even in this there is a tragic side. The nation is to be reborn still in unbelief and it is prophesied that Israel will experience the greatest persecution of its long history before it acknowledges its need of Christ for salvation. This has not yet come, but one can even now see the handwriting on the wall as Israel continues to defy and anger the Arab and Communist nations.

There are abundant references in Scripture to certain great coalitions of nations in the last days and to tremendous destructive wars between these groups. One group is centered in the Far East, one in the North (see Daniel 11:44; Revelation 16:12; Ezekiel 38); a third seems to consist of the Mediterranean and Atlantic nations and it is the latter which is the special subject of much of biblical prophecy. Over this group, a great popular leader is to arise and to be given vast dictatorial powers. Eventually, he is to gain control over the entire world (Revelation 13:7; Daniel 7:23).

There are many indications today that these outlined events may soon begin to take place. It is becoming more and more a matter of popular belief, as well as political propaganda, that the only hope for the world lies in a world government, with control of nuclear energy and other means of annihilative warfare. Especially if another "birth-pang"—a world war with all its terrible implications—should come, there is great likelihood that the outcome would be world federation and dictatorship.

But the Scriptures prophesy more than great political power being vested in this coming dictator. He will actually demand and receive worship as God himself, but he will not be God. He will be an evil man, speaking lies and blasphemies, and conducting relentless persecution against all who would worship the true God and his Christ (see Revelation 13). It is he who will loose the great persecution on the Jews when they also refuse to worship him as God.

The state of mind whereby men will be willing to worship a man, or group of men, as divine, is now rapidly being developed in the world. There is great emphasis today, in the intellectual world especially, upon the divinity of man. God is seen pantheistically as a great force, or principle, comprising all nature. He is thus identified with his creation, and is thought to be developing with it and only expressible in terms of it. Man, as the pinnacle of this "creation," is thus not only a part of God, but is actually that medium through which God manifests himself, through which he becomes mentally and spiritually alive. This is essentially the doctrine of humanism, which dominates the American educational, scientific and political establishments today.

These and similar views are being promoted by many today and are very appealing as they cater both to man's religious instincts and to his own pride and desire for independence from a personal, omnipotent, holy God.

The modern world has already seen acceptance and popular adulation of such evil, pseudo-divine dictators as Hitler, Mussolini, Stalin and Mao Tse-tung. Great numbers of people have worshiped them practically as gods, so it is not too difficult to foresee these events developing in the near future.

Thus, almost every important characteristic of our times is strong testimony to the prophetic truth of the Word of God, and to the imminence of Christ's return and the great world judgments accompanying. One more sign needs to be mentioned, different in character from all the others, which we have seen to be related to the dangers and evils and fears of the period at the end of this age.

When Christ ascended from this earth back to Heaven, he left his Church with one great aim and duty, that of going into all the world, and preaching "the gospel to every creature" (Mark 16:15). He said: "Ye shall be witnesses unto me. . .unto the uttermost part of the earth" (Acts 1:8). The first century church in large measure accomplished this commission, at least with reference to the known world at that time. However, the task was not complete, and each succeeding generation seemed to fall further behind in its duty of world evangelization. For century upon century, there was little or no missionary expansion of simple biblical Christianity. The modern missionary movement, largely beginning in the 19th century has, however, to a great extent (though far from what it ought to have been) changed this picture.

This modern missionary emphasis resulted largely from a return to biblical Christianity on the part of sizable groups of true Christians in the past two centuries. At the cost of much devotion, sacrifice, and prayer, Christ has been made known to people in most of the unevangelized lands of the earth, and some in nearly every such land have received him as Savior.

Now this is very significant in view of the Great Commission, which was followed almost immediately by the angelic promise to the disciples of Christ's bodily return (Acts 1:11), by implication, at the time when the commissioned task was completed. It attains added significance in light of the statement of our Lord in his great prophetic discourse on the Mount of Olives: "This gospel of the kingdom shall be preached in all the world for a witness unto all nations; and then shall the end come" (Matthew 24:14).

Some would limit this "gospel of the kingdom" to a special message applicable only during the coming period of the great tribulation. However, in all ages, men have entered the kingdom of God only by the new birth (John 3:3), on the basis of the sacrificial death of the Son of God, and this must be true in any coming age as well. Therefore, the gospel of the kingdom is another name for the "everlasting gospel" (Revelation 14:6) of God's grace in Jesus Christ, and when it has been preached for a witness to all nations, the "consummation" shall come.

Obviously, this prophecy is not yet completely fulfilled. There are still countries in which no real witness has yet been established, such as Tibet, Nepal, and Afghanistan. Many tribes in the jungles of Africa and South America are yet unreached. Even in those countries which have been objects of the greatest missionary effort, such as China and India, there are multitudes of villages without a Gospel testimony.

Revelation 7:9 speaks of a great multitude of all nations and kindreds and peoples and tongues in heaven redeemed by the blood of the Lamb. Just to what extent the objective of worldwide witnessing has been accomplished is a matter of some uncertainty, of course, as far as the interpretation of these Scriptures is concerned. It seems likely, however, that it is not yet complete (otherwise, Christ would have already come), but it also seems likely that it must nearly be so. Even the unreached peoples will probably soon have a Gospel witness. The work of Scripture translation, as well as pioneer mission work, is being pushed rapidly by numerous evangelical boards. The rapidly expanding use of modern inventions such as the radio and airplane is speeding the spread of the Gospel in many

There are thus many encouraging aspects about the mission situation. But still the great number of the unevangelized in all parts of the world stands as a tremendous indictment of and a tremendous challenge to the Church of Jesus Christ. Peter speaks of the possibility of "hasting unto the coming of the day of God" (II Peter 3:12), and it seems likely that this is a reference to the unfinished task of world evangelization, for God is long-suffering and desires that all men should come to repentance.

Thus, as the world deteriorates and ripens for judgment, the Gospel of Christ is nevertheless being taken to the ends of the earth—and all these things verify the truth of Scripture and suggest that the return of Christ may be very near.

For those who know him as Savior and Lord, his coming is the Blessed Hope. We long for his coming, and desire to hasten it if possible. Let us therefore, by intelligent witnessing and by holy lives yielded to him, try in every way we can to win men to acceptance of Christ as Savior; even more, let us do all we possibly can to get out the good tidings of salvation to those around the world who have never heard. Furthermore, we should urgently seek to bring our educational, social and political institutions back to recognition of the true God as Creator and Ruler of all things, so that the great masses of mankind will have greater reason to recognize Christ as Savior.

But for the reader who does not yet know the joy of assured salvation, may I urge him with all earnestness to receive the Lord Jesus as personal Savior. "For God so loved the world, that he gave his only begotten Son, that whosoever believeth in him should not perish, but have everlasting life" (John 3:16).

"Behold, *now* is the accepted time; behold *now* is the day of salvation" (II Corinthians 6:2).

SELECT BIBLIOGRAPHY

Chapter 2

Aalders, G. C. *The Problem of the Book of Jonah*. London: Tyndale, 1949.

Benson, Clarence H. *The Greatness and Grace of God*. Wheaton, Illinois: Scripture Press, 1953.

Brown, Arthur I. *Footprints of God*. Wheaton, Illinois: Van Kampen Press, 1943.

_____. *Miracles of Science*. Findlay, Ohio: Dunham, 1945.

Chestnut, D. Lee. *The Atom Speaks*. Grand Rapids: Eerdmans, 1951.

Clark, M. E. *Our Amazing Circulatory System—by Chance or Creation?* San Diego: Creation-Life Publishers, 1976.

Clark, Robert E. D. *The Universe: Plan or Accident?* London: Paternoster Press, 1949.

Coder, S. Maxwell, and Howe, George F. *The Bible, Science and Creation*. Chicago: Moody Press, 1966.

Davidheiser, Bolton. *Science and the Bible*. Grand Rapids: Baker, 1971.

De Vries, John. *Beyond the Atom*. Grand Rapids: Eerdmans, 1948.

Dolphin, Lambert. *Lord of Time and Space*. Westchester, Illinois: Good News, 1974.

Gish, Duane T., and Morris, Henry M. *The Battle for Creation*. San Diego: Creation-Life Publishers, 1976.

Hills, Edward F. *Space Age Science*. Des Moines: Christian Research, 1964.

Institute for Creation Research. *Twenty-One Scientists Who Believe in Creation*. San Diego: Creation-Life Publishers, 1977.

Lewis, C. S. *Miracles*. New York: Collins, 1947.

McMillen, S. I. *None of These Diseases*. Westwood, New Jersey: Revell, 1963.

Morris, Henry M. *Biblical Cosmology and Modern Science*. Nutley, New Jersey: Craig Press, 1970.

_____. *Studies in the Bible and Science*. Philadelphia: Presbyterian and Reformed, 1966.

_____. *The Remarkable Birth of Planet Earth*. Minneapolis: Bethany Fellowship, 1972.

Rehwinkel, Alfred M. *The The Wonders of Creation*. Grand Rapids: Baker, 1974.

Rimmer, Harry. *The Harmony of Science and Scripture*. Grand Rapids: Eerdmans, 1976.

Rushdoony, Rousas J. *The Mythology of Science*. Nutley, New Jersey: Craig Press, 1967.

Schnabel, A. O. *Has God Spoken?* San Diego: Creation-Life Publishers, 1974.

Short, A. Rendle. *Wonderfully Made.* London: Paternoster Press, 1951.

Smith, A. E. Wilder. *God: To Be or Not to Be.* Stuttgart, West Germany: Telos-International, 1975.

Totten, C. A. L. *Joshua's Long Day.* Haverhill, Massachusetts: Destiny, 1941.

Warfield, Benjamin B. *Miracles.* Grand Rapids: Eerdmans, 1965.

Whitcomb, John C. *Origin of the Solar System.* Philadelphia: Presbyterian and Reformed, 1964.

Williams, Emmett L., and Mulfinger, George. *Physical Science for Christian Schools.* Greenville, South Carolina: Bob Jones University Press, 1974.

Wood, Nathan R. *The Secret of the Universe.* Grand Rapids: Eerdmans, 1955.

Woods, Andrew J. *The Center of the Earth.* San Diego: Creation-Life Publishers, 1972.

Chapter 3

Clark, Harold W. *Wonders of Creation.* Mountain View, California: Pacific Press, 1964.

Clark, Robert E. D. *Darwin: Before and After.* Chicago: Moody Press, 1967.

Coppedge, James. *Evolution: Possible or Impossible?* Grand Rapids: Zondervan, 1973.

Cousins, Frank W. *Fossil Man.* Hants, England: Evolution Protest Movement, 1966.

Culp, G. Richard. *Remember Thy Creator.* Grand Rapids: Baker, 1975.

Custance, Arthur C. *Genesis and Early Man.* Grand Rapids: Zondervan, 1975.

———. *Evolution or Creation?* Grand Rapids: Zondervan, 1976.

Davidheiser, Bolton. *Evolution and the Christian Faith.* Philadelphia: Presbyterian and Reformed, 1969.

Dewar, Douglas. *The Transformist Illusion.* Murfreesboro, Tennessee: De Hoff, 1955.

Epp, Theodore H. *The God of Creation.* Lincoln, Nebraska: Back to the Bible, 1972.

Gish, Duane T. *Evolution: the Fossils Say No.* San Diego: Creation-Life Publishers, 1972.

———. *Dinosaurs–Those Terrible Lizards.* San Diego: Creation-Life Publishers, 1977.

———. *Speculations and Experiments on the Origin of Life. A Critique.* San Diego: Creation-Life Publishers, 1972.

———, Morris, Henry M., and Hillestad, George. *Creation-Acts, Facts, Impacts.* San Diego: Creation-Life Publishers, 1974.

Klotz, John W. *Genes, Genesis and Evolution*. St. Louis: Concordia, 1955.

Lammerts, Walter E., ed. *Scientific Studies in Special Creation*. Philadelphia: Presbyterian and Reformed, 1971.

_____ ,ed.*Why Not Creation?* Philadelphia: Presbyterian and Reformed, 1970.

Levitt, Zola. *Creation: A Scientist's Choice*. Wheaton, Illinois: Victor Books, 1976.

MacBeth, Norman. *Darwin Retried*. Boston: Gambit, 1971.

Marsh, Frank L. *Life, Man and Time*. Escondido, California: Outdoor Pictures, Inc., 1967.

Moore, John N. *Questions and Answers on Evolution/Creation*. Grand Rapids: Baker, 1976.

_____ , and Slusher, Harold S. *Biology: A Search for Order in Complexity*. Grand Rapids: Zondervan, 1970.

Morris, Henry M. *Evolution and the Modern Christian*. Philadelphia: Presbyterian and Reformed, 1967.

_____ . *The Scientific Case for Creation*. San Diego: Creation-Life Publishers, 1977.

_____ . *The Troubled Waters of Evolution*. San Diego: Creation-Life Publishers, 1975.

Nelson, Byron C. *After Its Kind*. Minneapolis: Bethany Fellowship, 1967.

Smith, A. E. Wilder. *Man's Origin, Man's Destiny*. Wheaton, Illinois: Harold Shaw, 1968.

_____ . *The Creation of Life*. Wheaton, Illinois: Harold Shaw, 1968.

Tilney, A. G. *The Case Against Evolution*. Hants, England: Evolution Protest Movement, 1964.

Tinkle, William J. *God's Method in Creation*. Nutley, New Jersey: Craig Press, 1973.

_____ . *Heredity: A Study in Science and the Bible*. Grand Rapids: Zondervan, 1970.

Wysong, R. L. *The Creation-Evolution Controversy*. East Lansing, Michigan: Inquiry Press, 1976.

Chapter 4

Barnes, Thomas G. *The Origin and Destiny of the Earth's Magnetic Field*. San Diego: Creation-Life Publishers, 1976.

Clark, Harold W. *Fossils, Flood and Fire*. Escondido, California: Outdoor Pictures, Inc., 1968.

_____ . *Genesis and Science*. Nashville, Tennessee: Southern Publishing Company, 1967.

Coffin, Harold G. *Creation: Accident or Design?* Washington: Review and Herald, 1969.

Cook, Melvin A. *Prehistory and Earth Models*. London: Max Parrish, 1966.

Daly, Reginald. *Earth's Most Challenging Mysteries*. Nutley, New Jersey: Craig Press, 1972.

Fields, Weston W. *Unformed and Unfilled*. Nutley, New Jersey: Presbyterian and Reformed, 1976.

Gish, Duane T., and Morris, Henry M. *The Battle for Creation*. San Diego: Creation-Life Publishers. 1976.

Howe, George F., ed. *Speak to the Earth*. Nutley, New Jersey: Craig Press, 1975.

Marsh, Frank L. *Life, Man and Time*. Escondido, California: Outdoor Pictures, Inc., 1967.

Morris, Henry M., ed. *Scientific Creationism*. San Diego: Creation-Life Publishers, 1976.

————. *The Beginning of the World*. Denver: Accent Books, 1977.

————, and Whitcomb, John C. *The Genesis Flood*. Philadelphia: Presbyterian and Reformed, 1961.

Morris, John D. *Adventure on Ararat*. San Diego: Creation-Life Publishers, 1973.

————, and LaHaye, Tim F. *The Ark on Ararat*. Nashville: Thomas Nelson, 1976.

Nelson, Byron C. *The Deluge Story in Stone*. Minneapolis: Bethany Fellowship, 1968.

Patten, Donald W., ed. *Symposium on Creation, I, II, III, IV, V*. Grand Rapids: Baker, 1969, 1970, 1971, 1972, 1975.

————. *The Biblical Flood and the Ice Epoch*. Seattle: Pacific Meridian, 1966.

Price, George McCready. *Common-Sense Geology*. Mountain View, California: Pacific Press, 1946.

————. *Evolutionary Geology and the New Catastrophism*. Mountain View, California: Pacific Press, 1926.

————. *The New Geology*. Mountain View, California: Pacific Press, 1923.

Rehwinkel, Alfred A. *The Flood*. St. Louis: Concordia, 1951.

Slusher, Harold S. *Critique of Radiometric Dating*. San Diego: Creation-Life Publishers, 1973.

Watson, David C. C. *Myths and Miracles*. Sussex, England: Henry Walter, Ltd., 1976.

Whitcomb, John C. *The Early Earth*. Nutley, New Jersey: Craig Press, 1973.

————. *The World That Perished*. Nutley, New Jersey: Craig Press, 1973.

Whitney, Dudley J. *Face of the Deep*. New York: Vantage Press, 1955.

————. *Genesis Versus Evolution*. New York: Exposition Press, 1961.

Chapter 5

Adam, Ben. *The Origin of Heathendom.* Minneapolis: Bethany Fellowship, 1963.

Allis, Oswald T. *The Five Books of Moses.* Grand Rapids: Eerdmans, 1954.

_____ . *The Old Testament: Its Claims and Critics.* Grand Rapids: Baker, 1972.

Bruce, F. F. *Are the New Testament Documents Reliable?* Grand Rapids: Eerdmans, 1954.

Courville, Donovan. *The Exodus Problem and Its Ramifications.* Loma Linda, California: Challenge Books, 1971.

Custance, Arthur C. *Noah's Three Sons.* Grand Rapids: Zondervan, 1975.

Davis, John J. *Conquest and Crisis.* Grand Rapids: Baker, 1969.

_____ . *Moses and the Gods of Egypt.* Grand Rapids: Baker, 1976.

Duffield, Guy P. *Handbook of Bible Lands.* Glendale, California: Regal Books, 1969.

Free, Joseph P. *Archaeology and Bible History.* Wheaton, Illinois: Scripture Press, 1950.

Greenleaf, Simon. *The Testimony of the Evangelists.* Grand Rapids: Baker, 1965.

Harris, R. Laird. *Inspiration and Canonicity of the Bible.* Grand Rapids: Zondervan, 1959.

Hyma, Albert, and Stanton, Mary. *Streams of Civilization.* San Diego: Creation-Life Publishers, 1976.

La Sor, William S. *The Dead Sea Scrolls and the New Testament.* Grand Rapids: Eerdmans, 1972.

Machen, J. Gresham. *The Virgin Birth of Christ.* New York: Harper, 1930.

McDowell, Josh. *More Evidence That Demands a Verdict.* Arrowhead Springs, California: Campus Crusade for Christ, 1974.

Montgomery, John W. *History and Christianity.* Downer's Grove, Illinois: Inter-Varsity Press, 1965.

Morris, Henry M. *The Genesis Record.* Grand Rapids: Baker, 1976.

Morrison, Frank. *Who Moved the Stone?* New York: Barnes and Noble, 1962.

Pfeiffer, Charles F. *The Dead Sea Scrolls and the Bible.* Grand Rapids: Baker, 1976.

Ramsay, William. *The Bearing of Recent Discovery on the Trustworthiness of the New Testament.* Grand Rapids: Baker, 1963.

Rushdoony, Rousas J. *The Biblical Philosophy of History.* Nutley, New Jersey: Presbyterian and Reformed, 1969.

Schwantes, Siegfried J. *The Biblical Meaning of History.* Mountain View, California: Pacific Press, 1970.

Smith, Wilbur. *The Supernaturalness of Christ.* Boston: W. A. Wilde Co., 1944.

Thompson, J. A. *The Bible and Archaeology.* Grand Rapids: Eerdmans, 1962.

Unger, Merrill F. *Archaeology and the New Testament.* Grand Rapids: Zondervan, 1962.

——— . *Archaeology and the Old Testament.* Grand Rapids: Zondervan, 1954.

Whitcomb, John C. *Darius the Mede.* Grand Rapids: Eerdmans, 1959.

——— . *Solomon to the Exile.* Grand Rapids: Baker, 1971.

Wilson, Clifford. *Ebla Tablets: Secrets of a Forgotten City.* San Diego: Creation-Life Publishers, 1977.

——— . *Exploring Bible Backgrounds.* Melbourne: Australian Institute of Archaeology, 1970.

——— . *The Passover Plot Exposed.* San Diego: Creation-Life Publishers, 1977.

Wilson, Robert Dick. *A Scientific Investigation of the Old Testament.* Chicago: Moody Press, 1959.

Wiseman, P. J. *New Discoveries in Babylonia about Genesis.* London: Marshall, Morgan and Scott, 1946.

Zwerner, Samuel M. *The Origin of Religion.* New York: Loizeaux, 1945.

Chapter 6

Anderson, Robert. *The Coming Prince.* Grand Rapids: Kregel, 1954.

Bullinger, E. W. *Number in Scripture.* London: The Lamp Press, Ltd., 1952.

Cooke, A. Earnest. *Fulfilled Prophecy.* Chicago: Moody Press, 1963.

Cooper, David L. *Messiah: His First Coming Scheduled.* Los Angeles: Biblical Research Society, 1939.

Davis, George T. B. *Bible Prophecies Fulfilled Today.* Philadelphia: Million Testaments Campaign, 1955.

Day, Gwynn M. *The Wonder of the Word.* New York: Revell, 1957.

De Hoff, George W. *Alleged Bible Contradictions Explained.* Murfreesboro, Tennessee: De Hoff Publications, 1970.

Engelder, Theodore. *The Scripture Cannot Be Broken.* St. Louis: Concordia, 1944.

Habershom, Ada R. *The Study of the Types.* Grand Rapids: Kregel, 1959.

Hamilton, Floyd E. *The Basis of Christian Faith.* New York: Harper, 1946.

Hull, William L. *The Fall and Rise of Israel.* Grand Rapids: Zondervan, 1954.

Kinney, LeBaron W. *The Greatest Thing in the Universe*. New York: Loizeaux, 1939.

Lang, G. H. *The Parabolic Teaching of Scripture*. Grand Rapids: Eerdmans, 1955.

Lightner, Robert P. *The Saviour and the Scriptures*. Nutley, New Jersey: Presbyterian and Reformed, 1970.

Linton, Irwin H. *A Lawyer Examines the Bible*. Grand Rapids: Baker, 1976.

Marsh, F. E. *The Structural Principles of the Bible*. Fincastle, Virginia: Bible Study Classics, n.d.

McDowell, Josh. *Evidence That Demands a Verdict*. Arrowhead Springs, California: Campus Crusade for Christ, 1972.

Morris, Henry M. *Many Infallible Proofs*. San Diego: Creation-Life Publishers, 1974.

Newell, Philip R. *Daniel–the Man Greatly Beloved and His Prophecies*. Chicago: Moody Press, 1962.

Rimmer, Harry. *Internal Evidences of Inspiration*. Grand Rapids: Eerdmans, 1938.

Rowell, Earle Albert. *Prophecy Speaks*. Takoma Park, Maryland: Review and Herald, 1933.

Stewart, Herbert. *The Stronghold of Prophecy*. London: Marshall, Morgan and Scott, 1941.

Stoner, Peter. *Science Speaks*. Chicago: Moody Press, 1952.

Urquhart, John. *Wonders of Prophecy*. London: Pickering and Inglis, 1949.

Warfield, Benjamin B. *The Inspiration and Authority of the Bible*. Philadelphia: Presbyterian and Reformed, 1948.

Watts, Newman. *The Incomparable Book*. Philadelphia: American Tract Society, 1940.

Wilson, Robert Dick. *Studies in the Book of Daniel*. New York: Revell, 1938.

Woods, T. E. P. *The Seal of the Seven*. Grand Rapids: Eerdmans, 1939.

Young, Edward J. *Thy Word is Truth*. Grand Rapids: Eerdmans, 1957.

Chapter 7
Anderson, J. N. D. *Christianity: the Witness of History*. London: Tyndale Press, 1969.

_____. *The World's Religions*. London: Inter-Varsity, 1950.

Anderson, Robert. *The Lord from Heaven*. Wheaton, Illinois: Van Kampen Press, n.d.

Bellett, J. G. *The Moral Glory of the Lord Jesus Christ*. New York: Loizeaux, 1943.

Brown, Colin. *Philosophy and the Christian Faith*. Downer's Grove, Illinois: Inter-Varsity Press, 1968.

Chapman, Colin. *Christianity on Trial*. Wheaton, Illinois: Tyndale House, 1974.

Clark, Gordon H. *Religion, Reason and Revelation*. Philadelphia: Presbyterian and Reformed, 1961.

Custance, Arthur C. *Man in Adam and in Christ*. Grand Rapids: Zondervan, 1975.

Denney, James. *The Death of Christ*. London: Inter-Varsity Press, 1951.

Guillebaud, H. E. *Some Moral Difficulties of the Bible*. London: Inter-Varsity Fellowship, 1941.

Hart-Davies, D. E. *The Severity of God*. London: Pickering and Inglis, 1946.

Krummacher, F. W. *The Suffering Saviour*. Chicago: Moody Press, 1948.

Lewis, C. S. *Mere Christianity*. New York: Macmillan, 1960.

––––––. *The Case for Christianity*. New York: Macmillan, 1948.

––––––. *The Problem of Pain*. New York: Macmillan, 1944.

Little, Paul E. *Know Why You Believe*. Wheaton, Illinois: Scripture Press, 1968.

Morris, Henry M. *Education for the Real World*. San Diego: Creation-Life Publishers, 1977.

Clark, Martin E. *The Bible Has the Answer*. San Diego: Creation-Life Publishers, 1976.

Orr, James. *The Christian View of God and the World*. Grand Rapids: Eerdmans, 1948.

Packer, J. I. *Evangelism and the Sovereignty of God*. Grand Rapids: Eerdmans, 1961.

Pinnock, Clark H. *Set Forth Your Case*. Nutley, New Jersey: Craig Press, 1968.

Rice, John R. *Is Jesus God?* Murfreesboro, Tenn.: The Sword of the Lord, 1966.

Schaeffer, Francis A. *How Should We Then Live?* Old Tappan, New Jersey: Revell, 1976.

––––––. *The God Who Is There*. Chicago: Inter-Varsity, 1968.

Seiss, Joseph A. *The Gospel in the Stars*. Grand Rapids: Kregel, 1972.

Sheldrake, Leonard. *Our Lord Jesus Christ, a Plant of Renown*. Ft. Dodge, Iowa: Walterick, 1950.

Sire, James W. *The Universe Next Door*. Downer's Grove, Illinois: Inter-Varsity Press, 1976.

Smith, A. E. Wilder: *Why Does God Allow It?* London: Victory Press, 1960.

Smith, Wilbur. *Therefore Stand*. Boston: W. A. Wilde, 1945.

Spencer, Duane E. *Mazzaroth.* San Antonio: Word of Grace, 1972.

Strombeck, J. F. *So Great Salvation.* Strombeck Agency: n.p., 1942.

Thomas, W. H. Griffith. *Christianity is Christ.* London: Church Book Room Press, 1948.

Warfield, Benjamin B. *The Plan of Salvation.* Grand Rapids: Eerdmans, 1935.

Wenham, John W. *The Goodness of God.* Downers Grove, Illinois: Inter-Varsity Press, 1974.

Wood, Nathan R. *The Open Secret of Christianity.* New York: Revell, 1950.

Chapter 8

Andrews, Samuel J. *Christianity and Anti-Christianity in Their Final Conflict.* Chicago: Moody Press, 1937.

Brown, Arthur I. *The Eleventh Hour.* Wheaton, Illinois: Van Kampen Press. 1947.

Cooper, David L. *Future Events Revealed.* Los Angeles: Biblical Research Society, 1940.

Feinberg, Charles L., ed. *Jesus the King is Coming.* Chicago: Moody Press, 1975.

Lacey, Harry. *God and the Nations.* New York: Loizeaux, 1942.

LaHaye, Tim F. *The Beginning of the End.* Wheaton, Illinois: Tyndale House, 1972.

Lindsey, Hal. *The Late Great Planet Earth.* Grand Rapids: Zondervan, 1970.

Morris, Henry M. *The Twilight of Evolution.* Grand Rapids: Baker, 1964.

Pentecost, J. Dwight. *Things to Come.* Findlay, Ohio: Dunham, 1958.

Price, Walter K. *In the Final Days.* Chicago: Moody Press, 1977.

––––––. *Next Year in Jerusalem.* Chicago: Moody Press, 1977.

––––––. *The Coming of Anti-Christ.* Chicago: Moody Press, 1973.

Ryrie, Charles C. *The Bible and Tomorrow's News.* Wheaton, Illinois: Scripture Press, 1969.

––––––. *The Living End.* Old Tappan, New Jersey: Revell, 1976.

Smith, Wilbur M. *Egypt in Biblical Prophecy.* Boston: W. A. Wilde, 1957.

––––––. *Israeli-Arab Conflict and the Bible.* Glendale, California: Gospel Light, 1967.

––––––. *This Atomic Age and the Word of God.* Boston: W. A. Wilde, 1948.

––––––. *World Crises and the Prophetic Scriptures.* Chicago: Moody Press, 1951.

Tatford, Frederick. *The Clock Strikes.* Ft. Washington, Pennsylvania: Christian Literature Crusade, 1972.

Walvoord, John F. *The Nations in Prophecy*. Grand Rapids: Zondervan, 1967.

Wilson, Clifford. *Crash Go the Chariots*. San Diego: Creation-Life Publishers, 1976.

———. *The Occult Explosion*. San Diego: Creation-Life Publishers, 1976.